Contents

Windows of Opportunity

PUBLIC POLICY AND THE POOR

Edited by Saul Becker

CPAG Ltd, 1-5 Bath Street, London EC1V 9PY

CPAG promotes action for the relief, directly or indirectly, of poverty among children and families with children. We work to ensure that those on low incomes get their full entitlements to welfare benefits. In our campaigning and information work we seek to improve benefits and policies for low-income families, in order to eradicate the injustice of poverty. If you are not already supporting us, please consider a donation, or ask for details of our membership schemes and publications.

Published by CPAG Ltd
1-5 Bath Street, London EC1V 9PY

© CPAG Ltd 1991

ISBN 0 946744 35 1

The views expressed in this book are the authors' and do not necessarily reflect those of CPAG.

Poverty Publication 81

Cover and design by Devious Designs, 0742-755634
Cover photographic credits (from top left clockwise): Joanne O'Brien, Brenda Prince, Judy Harrison, Brenda Prince
Typeset by Nancy White, 071-607 4510
Printed by Blackmore Press, 0747-53034

List of Tables

Acknowledgements

Many people helped in the preparation of this book. CPAG's staff and friends worked hard to produce the book to very tight deadlines. Members of CPAG's publications sub-committee made valuable comments on the initial book proposal. Particular thanks must go to Fran Bennett and Julia Lewis who commented on early drafts of the manuscript and to Julia Lewis for her work on the production of the book. All the contributors promptly delivered their chapters, despite their very full timetables. David Piachaud, Carey Oppenheim, David Bull and Robin Simpson read and commented on individual chapters. Margot Lunnon read the manuscript as a whole. I owe a particular debt to Ruth Lister, who worked through all the draft chapters and made invaluable comments and suggestions. The highly professional work of Peter Ridpath on the promotion of the book and Debbie Haynes' well-known ability to distribute finished copies at breakneck pace will both make an invaluable contribution to its success. Finally, thanks also to all the other people, including Vivian Dhaliwal, Ann Smith, Peter Beaman and Mavis Hearnden, who worked behind the scenes, and whose help has been very much appreciated.

Saul Becker, August 1991

About the contributors

Pete Alcock is Principal Lecturer in Social Policy at Sheffield City Polytechnic and a member of CPAG's Executive Committee.

Dr Saul Becker is Director of Studies for the multidisciplinary masters degree in Policy, Organisation and Change in Professional Care at the University of Loughborough.

Fran Bennett is the Director of the Child Poverty Action Group.

Alan Deacon is Professor of Social Policy at the University of Leeds.

Peter Golding is Professor of Sociology and Head of the Department of Social Sciences at the University of Loughborough. He is a member of CPAG's Executive Committee.

Paul Gordon is a Research and Information Officer with the Runnymede Trust. His most recent publications include *Citizenship for Some: Race and Government Policy 1979-89* and *Fortress Europe? The Meaning of 1992*.

Dr Jane Millar is Reader in Social Policy at the University of Bath. Her recent books include *Lone Parent Families in the UK* (with Jonathan Bradshaw) and *Women and Poverty in Britain* (co-edited with Caroline Glendinning).

Dr Graham Room is Reader in Social Policy at the University of Bath and Director of the Centre for Research in European Social and Employment Policy.

Peter Townsend is Professor of Social Policy at the University of Bristol and Honorary President of CPAG.

Dr Jill Vincent is a Research Fellow in the Centre for Research in Social Policy, Dept of Social Sciences, University of Loughborough.

Foreword
International windows

Peter Townsend

THIS book calls for nothing less than a transformation in policies for people in poverty. Although the contributors necessarily confine themselves to what needs to be done for the poorest quarter or third of the population of the United Kingdom, such redistributive policies need increasingly to be addressed on an international scale.

This represents a daunting, and quite complex, programme of political education. There is no point in pretending it is just a question of perceptions, priorities, morality, party policies and organisation or votes. It is all of these things. Structures, and not merely attitudes, have to change – in the practical interests of the economy as a whole and of the rich and prosperous, as well as the impoverished minorities. Many people have to be persuaded to take a number of connected steps in the comprehension of the problem. The *first* step is a full recognition of the growing divide in the UK itself. These days no one questions the evidence of growing inequality of incomes and wealth. But at both ends of the spectrum the severity of the differences is grossly under-represented. At one end personal or corporate wealth, employer benefits and cash income are measured inadequately – or not at all. At the other, my calculations show that the real incomes of millions of people have actually declined since 1979 and the falls are concealed in the presentation of official statistics.

The full social effects of this change have to be absorbed. The emergence of a so-called 'underclass' cannot be separated from the corresponding emergence of an overclass. Certainly the class hierarchy is deeper – and more entrenched – than it was in the past. The growing divide of incomes is reflected in jobs and jobless, homes and homeless and citizens and stateless. It is also reflected in the deterioration in social relations and public trust and the steady rise in rates of violence, burglary and theft. In the Britain of the early 1990s there are many unacceptable, as well as ugly, manifestations of ageism, sexism and racism. It is not a pretty picture.

The *second* step is the better identification of cause. The problem is not one solely of the Thatcher governments' making – although those governments bear a huge responsibility for its growth in scale in the last twelve years. It is deeply located in Britain's colonial, imperialist and class traditions and powerful administrative and professional institutions which have been moulded by the policies of different governments over many years. It is also increasingly determined, and not merely controlled, by the rapid evolution of international agencies and organisations – multinational companies with empires extending to former communist states, a European Community with a long line of potential member states knocking on its doors, and bodies like the IMF, the World Bank, UNCTAD and the FAO wielding greatly enhanced powers. Since 1972, the UK government's power to act has been cirumscribed by European law. From 1992, the Single Market will further restrict any scope for independent national action.

Many people still underestimate the shift of power to multi-national conglomerates and the social consequences of that change. Yes, the Thatcher governments adopted policies of privatisation, deregulation, cuts in public expenditure, and devaluation of low incomes and public services, which have increased the extent of poverty and reduced the quality of life and opportunities of millions of people, in the mistaken belief that this would make Britain more economically competitive and more secure. But those governments actually embodied many of the values of the international market to which they owed increasing allegiance, and whose interests they served. Britain was going faster along the same road in scrapping public services and regulations and welfare subsidies than the other members of the European Community. National policies in the UK were dismantled without corresponding European replacement. For example, public employment subsidies on behalf of the unemployed in different regions have been wound down without any surge in the resources being deployed on behalf of social development in what can be characterised as the 'European' or 'international' welfare state.

The budgets allocated by the European Community for the Social Fund, the Anti-Poverty Programme and the implementation of the meagre provisions of the Social Charter are small and inadequate. Large-scale unemployment seems to be accepted as an inevitable phenomenon in the Europe of the 1990s and 2000s. Authoritarian policies to control people with non-resident, immigrant, visitor and refugee status are being devised. Two-tier Europe is one prospect. Internal poverty of a severity, and even a scale, comparable with much Third World poverty is another.

The *third* step in comprehending the new world in which all of us are unavoidably immersed is therefore to adopt an international, and not simply national, strategy for change. The political institutions of the European Community are far from being democratic. European company and other laws have to be promulgated to condition and influence the social policies of the multinationals. European social policy institutions have to be developed. A dual system of local or regional and European representation must be evolved to achieve a level of acceptable social stability. We must consciously strive for the evolution of an international welfare state.

I say 'international' and not 'European' in anticipation of taking a *fourth* step in comprehension of the problem. This is the need to offset the modern form of imperialism represented by the growth of the European Community. The cause of anti-poverty policies cannot be achieved without world-wide action and agreement. In the long run, policies which reek of 'devil take the hindmost' are never successful. Multinational companies are not restricted in their operations to Europe, and their control there will depend on their control elsewhere. Sooner or later regional and international development policies have to be given precedence over specifically European policies.

Finally, there is the practicality and not just desirability of the transformation for which UK governments and pressure groups must now work. Local support for such action exists and has to be tapped. Local consent is critical to success. Local confidence has to be built up at the same time as international planning is set in place. But the practicality of transformation also depends on appreciation of the immense resources which could be released by redistributive taxation and other measures. Even moderate restraints on the accumulation of extravagant levels of personal wealth could produce the resources to remove beggars from our streets.

1.
Introduction: from enterprise to opportunity

Saul Becker

Now that another election looms, it is the duty of CPAG, as well as something of a tradition – whichever party is seeking re-election – to examine the government's record in respect of the poor.
Alan Walker, *The Growing Divide*[1]

The state of poverty

CPAG's tradition of acting as witness and social commentator stretches back over twenty-five years.[2] More recently, *Thatcherism and the Poor* examined the record of the Conservative government of 1979-1983, and *The Growing Divide* extended the record to 1987. These books provide a detailed and meticulous analysis of government policies during the greater part of the 1980s, and their impact on poor people in the United Kingdom.

The record is bleak. It reveals a rising tide of poverty and growing inequality. Taking one proxy for a measure of poverty[3] – the numbers living below half average income – in 1979, when Mrs Thatcher first came to power, just under 5 million people (or 9.4 per cent of the population of Great Britain) lived below half average income, after meeting housing costs. By 1983, the numbers had increased to 6.4 million (11.9 per cent of the population); by 1987, when Mrs Thatcher secured her third term, the numbers had rocketed to 10.5 million (19.4 per cent of the population).[4] The latest available figures show that by 1988 just under 12 million people – one in five of the population – lived in poverty, if defined in this way.[5]

The rise in the number of children forced to live in poverty is even starker than the growth in poverty generally. In 1979, about

1.6 million children lived in poor households (defined as living on incomes below half the average). By 1988, this figure had risen to 3 million children – a quarter of all children in Britain.[6] Figures such as these are frightening not just because of the numbers affected. It is the *experience* of poverty, obscured behind sanitised statistics, that also requires our attention, concern, anger and action. Millions of men, women and children in this country - but also, as we shall see, in the wider European Community[7] – live in a society in which they daily experience exclusion and 'partial citizenship'.[8] Poverty means powerlessness – a lack of voice, as well as political, economic and social marginalisation.[9] Poor people are denied access to many of the activities and services which are widely taken for granted. They experience the poverty of restricted opportunities and inhibited life chances for themselves and their children. In addition, the living standards of poor people are often so low that they are forced to go without the most basic of essentials, such as adequate housing, clothing and nutrition.[10] Children suffer in particular, with poverty casting its shadow forward over their lives. As Bradshaw notes, poverty amongst children is associated with low birth weight, low growth rates, high infant mortality and vulnerability to disability and illness.[11] Townsend concluded his chapter in *The Growing Divide* with the chilling statement, 'poverty damages health; poverty kills'.[12]

None of this is new to those who experience poverty every day, or those who work with, or campaign on behalf of, poor people. To these, the facts and reality of poverty are well known. But, to a large extent, in the 1980s poverty remained invisible, hidden from popular view, except when it spilled out on to the streets of our major cities and forced itself, at least for a time, into public consciousness. The word 'poverty' seemed to be deleted from official use for much of the decade. Certainly, as Chapter 4 shows, there was widespread toleration of public squalor amid private affluence, with a view that the 'poor are always with us', and that little could be done about them. And as Chapter 2 shows, these beliefs received support, and encouragement, from New Right thinking emerging in the United States, which defined poverty in terms of individual behaviour.[13] Beliefs such as these, refined to the point of ideology, seemed to influence the later years of the Thatcher governments in particular.[14]

Since the publication of *The Growing Divide* in 1987, the Conservatives have radically reformed the social security system in 1988 and the NHS in 1991 and have escalated their privatisation programme. Almost month by month one new policy initiative or another has affected people in poverty (see Appendix). This volume brings the analysis of Conservative policy up to the present. And with the change of Conservative leadership in 1990, this book is now able to evaluate the impact and legacy of the Thatcher years. But the ink is not yet dry on this particular chapter of our social and political history. Poor people have yet to experience the full impact of some of the Thatcher governments' later policies – the introduction of the NHS and community care reforms, the Child Support Act and disability benefit changes, to name but a few.

Do the Conservatives' proposals for the future offer new hope and real opportunities for poor people and particularly for children in poverty? While Mrs Thatcher may have eschewed collective Cabinet, the government cannot avoid collective responsibility for the last twelve years of Conservative power. The 1980s must surely be unique in the number and scope of reports on poverty and deprivation, published by a range of bodies and individuals from official and large-scale research units to solitary individuals working at the front line. Many of these efforts did not strike the right chord with policy-makers, and were treated disparagingly or ignored.[15] But the 1980s was also the decade of the failure of alternative argument and alternative vision, and of discord and division amongst the opposition parties for much of the period.[16]

So the time is ripe for a critical assessment of what the new Conservative government of John Major has to offer, and whether it differs to any large extent from the governments of his predecessor. And it is also time to assess what the main opposition parties have to impart, after so long outside government. The answers to these questions are vital to the future of people in poverty, and especially to the future of poor children – also to the future of our society as a whole, because one cannot be divorced from the other.

Structure and content of the book

Looking forward

Rather than simply focus on the Conservatives' record, our intention is also to define a new agenda for the 1990s, which would provide people in poverty with real windows of opportunity enabling them to participate as full citizens in society. The book therefore looks to the past and to the future. Chapters 2 to 4 review the values and principles underpinning recent social and economic policies and the impact of these policies on poor people during the 1980s. These chapters also identify the changing attitudes towards poverty and the poor during the decade. Chapter 5 charts the map of poverty in the European Community and identifies some future policy issues. Chapters 6 to 9 provide the foundations for discussion of a new agenda for public policy for the 1990s, based on the principles of rights, quality, citizenship, participation and opportunity. In addition, a number of these chapters focus on the implications for poor people of greater integration with Europe.

In our assessment of the Thatcher years, **Chapter 2** examines the central features of the approach to poverty and social security policy adopted by successive Conservative governments, before examining in greater detail the arguments advanced and policies pursued since 1987. (In short, this chapter picks up where *The Growing Divide* left off.) Thatcherism's particular approach to social policy is discussed, with its emphasis on the virtues of inequalities, repudiation of government responsibility for unemployment, privatisation policies and the restraint and control of public expenditure. Alan Deacon shows how, together, these driving principles led to a retreat from state welfare and the growth of private and voluntary provision, and goes on to warn of the dangers of exaggerating the changes brought about by the Conservatives' election of John Major as their new Prime Minister.

Chapter 3 identifies who bore the cost of these principles and policies. It charts the growth of poverty and inequality in the 1980s and identifies who gained the most from government policies, and who paid the price. Jane Millar discusses the main reasons for the increase in poverty during the period. In particular, she identifies a number of labour market trends – including the persistently high levels of unemployment and its unequal distribution, the rising incidence of low-paid work and the growth in precarious or flexible employment, concentrated especially amongst women. Government policies during the 1980s, Millar argues, exacerbated the impact of these trends. Finally, Millar focuses on social security policy and the manner in which the constant barrage of policy changes in the 1980s often worked against the interests and security of poor and low-income people.

Chapter 4 charts the changes and patterns of public attitudes towards poverty during the decade, using a number of major studies from this country and Europe. Peter Golding suggests that attitudes to poverty and people in poverty continue to display antipathy and hostility and are characterised by contradictions – despite some encouraging signs. Golding outlines a number of policy implications for the 1990s, and ways in which 'poor attitudes' can be influenced by those concerned with poverty and its prevention.

In **Chapter 5** Graham Room examines the major economic, demographic and social changes that are likely to take place during the 1990s as they relate to people living on low incomes. His focus is upon the UK, but seen in relation to the other countries of Western Europe, with which, as he says, this country is becoming increasingly integrated. Room charts the growth in the numbers of people living on relatively low incomes and receiving means-tested benefits, and the changing composition of the low-income population in the European Community as a whole. The chapter goes on to identify the main developments that are likely to change the map of poverty in the 1990s – in particular the ageing population, the increase in the numbers of lone parents and the likely rates and patterns of unemployment. Finally, the chapter illuminates the social policy options that could re-shape the map of poverty, especially at the European Community level. In particular, Room discusses the issue of which groups in poverty are likely to have policies defined for them at the level of the individual national state, and which will be dealt with at a Europe-wide level.

Chapter 6 provides a framework for the discussion of the future of welfare rights. By drawing on the development of welfare rights work over the last two decades – and specifically the challenges to rights posed by the Thatcher governments – Pete Alcock argues that rights to welfare, across the range of public, private and voluntary services, are likely to be a central issue in policy development in the 1990s. Alcock goes on to show how rights, and in particular rights to quality welfare services, are an essential part of citizenship, and provide a much needed certainty in welfare provision – certainty in what users can expect, and in what providers should deliver to a particular standard. This certainty should displace discretion and professional control, and the paternalism of much post-war state welfare. By providing enforceable rights to quality standards of welfare across all sectors, Alcock believes that welfare rights will also counter the threat that public services could increasingly become poor quality services, for all the promise of the Citizen's Charter. The chapter goes on to consider a number of key issues, including the role that service users themselves can play in developing rights; the need for a commitment to new thinking and a new set of priorities – such as a reduction in the use of means-testing and a recast 'social insurance' scheme whereby individuals are provided with security without a test of means, and without traditional contribution tests.

Chapter 7 takes up the theme of citizenship, but shows how, in its current narrow legal sense, the concept has worked to exclude black people from the rights of social citizenship through immigration and nationality legislation, racism and poverty. The chapter goes on to examine the implications for black people of the 'new Europe'. Paul Gordon shows how the new Europe coming into being is built on exclusion, on citizenship for some but not for all. What is needed, he argues, is a genuinely pluralist and more embracing form of citizenship, which welcomes difference as a positive fact of contemporary life.

Chapter 8 provides a detailed and critical examination of the main Parliamentary political parties' positions on poverty. What is each offering people in poverty in the run-up to, and beyond, the general election? The answers provide the political starting-point for the future of anti-poverty policies in the 1990s. Fran Bennett focuses first on current Conservative concerns, and the apparent differences of emphasis between Prime Minister John Major's agenda and that of his predecessor. Bennett then goes on to examine both the Labour and Liberal Democrats' positions. She assesses to what extent the parties will provide real opportunities for everyone to participate as full citizens in society.

Chapter 9 identifies how public policy can promote opportunities and rights of social citizenship for all. Becker and Bennett provide the foundations for a discussion of a new agenda; they focus on the creation of employment opportunities, changes in taxation policy and improvements in services, and, as befits a CPAG publication, they pay particular attention to changes in social security policy. By providing both concrete statements of principle on which policy should be based, and specific examples of policy changes, Becker and Bennett call for politicians of all parties to develop the political will and comprehensive strategy, and for the public as a whole to develop a commitment, to bring about freedom from poverty, and to provide windows of opportunity for all.

From enterprise to opportunity

For people in poverty, the Thatcher years were largely a decade of lost opportunities. Economic policy undermined the objectives of social policy, and the result was greater poverty and exclusion for millions of citizens.[17] But there does appear now to be a shift in the rhetoric of the three main political parties, to a shared middle ground. All are promoting the consumer's right to quality services, in particular in the public sector.[18] Both the Conservatives[19] and Labour[20] emphasise 'opportunity' as the theme for the future. There is, as Fran Bennett argues in Chapter 8, a greater emphasis on 'fairness' in public policy. Yet both the Conservatives and Labour still maintain that progress in extending opportunity and fairness is dependent on the timing of economic recovery. But poor people have waited long enough. If the social objectives of an opportunity society, a fair society, are made subordinate to the traditional goals of economic policy, then the 1990s are set to be another decade of lost opportunities for the poor; a decade where public policy continues to deny poor people real opportunities to participate as full citizens in our society.

Notes

1. A Walker, 'Introduction: A policy for two nations', in A Walker and C Walker (eds), *The Growing Divide: A Social Audit 1979-1987*, CPAG Ltd, 1987, p1.
2. See, for example, CPAG, *Poverty and the Labour Government*, 1970; D Bull and P Wilding (eds), *Thatcherism and the Poor*, CPAG, 1983; A Walker and C Walker, *see* note 1.
3. C Oppenheim, *Poverty: The Facts*, CPAG Ltd, 1990.
4. Social Security Committee, *Low Income Statistics: Households Below Average Income: Tables 1988*, HMSO, 1991. *See* also Chapter 3.
5. *See* note 4.
6. *See* note 4.
7. See, for example, Chapters 5 and 7.
8. Peter Golding has argued that poverty 'is most comprehensively understood as a condition of partial citizenship': P Golding (ed), *Excluding the Poor*, CPAG, 1986, pxi. See also R Lister, *The Exclusive Society: Citizenship and the Poor*, CPAG Ltd, 1990.
9. A meeting at York in 1990 brought together people with experience of poverty and people involved 'professionally' in campaigning against poverty. The purpose was to see 'how people in poverty could become more involved in anti-poverty campaigning and thereby gain greater control over their own lives': R Lister and P Beresford, *Working Together against Poverty*, Open Services

Project/Department of Applied Social Studies, Bradford University, 1991.

10. For a recent survey see: National Children's Home, *Children in Danger 1991: Family Nutrition Survey*, NCH, 1991. *See* also Chapter 3.

11. J Bradshaw, *Child Poverty and Deprivation in the UK*, National Children's Bureau, 1990.

12. P Townsend, 'Poor health', in A Walker and C Walker, *see* note 1, p87.

13. See, for example, C Murray, *Losing Ground*, Basic Books, 1984; and L Mead, *Beyond Entitlement*, Free Press, 1986.

14. Alan Deacon argues in Chapter 2 that New Right thinking from the USA was particularly influential on John Moore, Secretary of State for Social Services (and, later, Social Security).

15. There are many examples of this. However, perhaps the most persistent is the barrage of critical research studies, from 1988 onwards, on the operation of the discretionary social fund. The government still maintains the fund is 'a great success'. See S Becker and R Silburn, *The New Poor Clients*, Community Care/Benefits Research Unit, 1990.

16. In his biography of Margaret Thatcher, Hugo Young argues, 'The absence of an effective parliamentary opposition was central to a great deal of what happened throughout the decade from 1979... Labour and the Liberals and the SDP were destined to thrash about in a state of abject confusion.' Young suggests that this state of affairs confirmed to many Thatcherites that there was 'no conceivable basis for another sort of politics': H Young, *One of Us*, Macmillan, 1989, pp530-31.

17. See, for example, D Piachaud, 'The god that failed', *The Guardian*, 31 July 1991.

18. '...I am determined to give power back to the people who use public services ... there must no longer be any hiding place for sloppy standards, lame excuses and attitudes that patronise the public', Rt Hon John Major MP, quoted in *The Independent*, 11 May 1991. See also *The Citizen's Charter: Raising the Standard*, HMSO, Cmnd 1599, July 1991; and *Opportunity Britain: Labour's Better Way into the 1990s*, April 1991.

19. The themes of the Conservatives' election campaign will be 'individual opportunities and responsibilities, caring for those who cannot look after themselves ... and a vigorous enterprise society with excellence in the public services', quoted in *The Independent*, 20 May 1991.

20. '...if individuals are to flourish and society to thrive in freedom, people need the means to develop their potential... That is the essence of modern democratic socialism ... with its core conviction of liberty, justice and opportunity for all...', Rt Hon Neil Kinnock MP, quoted in *The Guardian*, 16 April 1991. See also *Opportunity Britain: Labour's Better Way into the 1990s*, April 1991.

2.
The retreat from state welfare

Alan Deacon

THERE is broad agreement amongst observers that the Thatcher governments of 1979-90 marked a decisive break in British politics. In part, this is seen as a question of *personality*. For much of her premiership, Mrs Thatcher was able to dominate the Cabinet – and manipulate the lobby system – far more than her predecessors. In part, it is viewed as a change in the *style of government* and more than a decade of Mrs Thatcher's 'conviction politics' has done much to undermine the previously fashionable belief that British government was becoming inexorably more corporatist in nature. Above all, however, Thatcherism is seen as an *ideology*. As such, its distinctiveness is held to lie in a fusion of two hitherto separate strands: conservative populism with its stress on nation, defence and law, and liberal political economy with its emphasis upon individualism and the superiority of a market order.

The present chapter does not try to summarise the burgeoning literature on Thatcherism. Instead, it discusses briefly the central features of the approach to poverty and social security policy adopted by successive Thatcher governments, before examining more closely the arguments advanced and policies pursued since 1987.

The approach to social policy

The acceptance of inequalities

The overriding emphasis given to the *creation* of wealth, and the effective denial of government responsibility for its *distribution,* are central themes in the Thatcher governments' approach to social policy. The task of government, so the argument goes, is to ensure a national minimum, above which the distribution of resources will be determined by market outcomes. As Gamble noted, in a social market economy 'social justice resides not in what individuals get, but in the rules governing how they get it. In return for economic liberty, individuals must reconcile themselves to great and often arbitrary inequalities.'[1]

For the Thatcher governments, intervention to reduce inequalities would constitute an unwarranted interference in individual freedom. It would also be counter-productive, since such intervention would invariably impede the market and thereby reduce economic growth. The converse was equally true. Not only would a properly functioning market economy generate far more wealth than a more planned economy, but that wealth would also eventually be spread throughout the labour force. Although income differentials might widen, in absolute terms the lowest paid would still be better off. This 'trickle-down' effect was as certain as night follows day, and, if it did not show up in the official statistics, then there was obviously something wrong with the statistics.

This, of course, left open the question of the *level* of the minimum, especially for those not in work and dependent on benefits. Clearly, the minimum could not rise in line with the growth in national income. Such a relative standard would make it impossible to restrain spending on benefits effectively in order to deliver tax cuts as promised, and would also undermine work incentives. Thus, as early as 1980, the government cut the link between earnings and long-term benefits, and, temporarily, reduced the real level of unemployment and sickness benefits. For most of the 1980s, the major benefits were increased broadly in line with prices. This meant of course that they – and the *de facto* minimum – fell further and further behind the growth in earnings.

The impact of this upon people on low incomes and claimants' living standards is examined in the following chapter, but it should be noted that the Thatcher government's oft-expressed confidence in the strategy did not extend to the ready publication of data with which its impact upon poverty could be assessed.[2] Indeed, in May 1989, John Moore, the Secretary of State for Social Security, made an extraordinary speech in which he appeared to deny that poor people existed at all. He went on to question the 'relative' nature of poverty:

> What basis in common sense is there for saying that somebody on
> 49 per cent of average earnings is any more in poverty than someone
> on 50 per cent, 51 per cent or even 100 per cent?

Neither, it seems, did common sense play any part in the 'political
definition' of poverty which had been developed in the 1960s. Moore
argued that 'language' had been 'shaped' and 'facts manipulated
deliberately' in order to present as 'poverty' what was 'in reality
simply inequality'. Moreover, this had all been done to make it
possible to call 'western material capitalism a failure'. It was, Moore
told his audience, 'one of the more fascinating and, until now, little
discussed political stories of our time':

> I suggest that what happened was that by the 1960s the gulf in living
> standards between countries under socialist governments and those
> with capitalist systems had become glaringly apparent... At this point
> of crisis for socialism, academics came to the rescue. Realising that
> poverty ... was on the wane, academics helpfully discovered a new
> kind of poverty.[3]

It is true, of course, that Moore's somewhat idiosyncratic interpretation
of history was not necessarily shared by all his colleagues – or even
perhaps by Mrs Thatcher, who sacked him two months later. The fact
remains, however, that the word 'poverty' was deleted from official
vocabulary and that the government continued to appear indifferent
to the distributional impact of its policies – a stance which was to
culminate in the introduction of the poll tax.

The repudiation of government responsibility for unemployment

The stagflation of the 1970s had a traumatic effect on economists and
politicians of all persuasions. It created a climate in which inflation
was almost universally regarded as a greater threat than unemployment. For the new leadership of the Conservative Party, however,
the crucial lesson of those years was that, in Sir Keith Joseph's words,
'Full employment is not in the gift of governments. It should not be
promised and it cannot be provided.'[4] According to the new
conventional wisdom, unemployment was primarily the result not of
a deficiency in the level of aggregate demand but of dysfunctions in
the labour market. Attempts to reduce it by higher public spending
would only lead to ever higher inflation. The task of government,

therefore, was to facilitate the working of the labour market, within which jobs would 'occur'. This should be done through a variety of measures, including education and training programmes designed to minimise the mismatch between the skills required by employers and those possessed by the jobless, and by reducing regional imbalances through steps to improve labour mobility.

It was argued that the central responsibility of government was to create a framework within which unemployed people would price themselves back into work by accepting jobs at market wages. This would require in turn a significant reduction in union power, the reduction of wages councils' powers and an overhaul of the structure of both taxation and benefits so as to increase work incentives. All of this would be accompanied by measures to promote an 'enterprise culture', in which risk-taking would be encouraged and initiative and effort rewarded.

Such 'supply-side' measures could be augmented by temporary job creation schemes targeted at particular groups, but otherwise there was little a government could do to influence the level of unemployment. It followed that a government which met its obligations in this respect could not be blamed if unemployment continued to rise, and the success of the Thatcher governments in persuading the electorate of this 'fact' was one of the most striking features of the decade. There are a number of reasons why unemployment appeared to lose its political significance, especially in the early 1980s. However, central to any explanation must be the concentration of unemployment in particular regions and on particular groups. Thus the effect of unemployment – as of widening inequalities generally – was to disadvantage severely a substantial minority while the majority enjoyed rising living standards, a process which Alan Walker has aptly termed the 'two-thirds/one-third' strategy.[5] Even so, unemployment remained a sensitive issue, and the government's preoccupation with data on poverty was echoed in a seemingly endless series of 'adjustments' to the unemployment statistics, the net effect of which was to reduce the headline total substantially.[6]

Privatisation

The more enthusiastic of Mrs Thatcher's supporters often emphasised what John Moore called the 'total consistency of the Conservative vision'.[7] An important part of this was the application to social policy of the attitudes and ideas which had been so 'successful' in the economic sphere. Pre-eminent amongst these was privatisation.

The term 'privatisation' has, of course, encompassed a wide range of measures in virtually all areas of social policy. In social security, it included the transfer to employers of responsibilities for the administration of statutory sick pay and maternity pay, and, less explicitly, a greater reliance upon voluntary bodies, in particular to meet the needs of those refused help from the social fund. The most important – and certainly the most costly – initiative has been the promotion of occupational and personal pensions.

The Social Security Act 1986 restricted the scope of the State Earnings Related Pension Scheme (SERPS) and introduced incentives for individuals to contract out of SERPS in favour of private provision through 'personal pensions'. The Department of Health and Social Security (as it was then called) had a working assumption that half a million people would take out a personal pension. In the event, however, the generosity of the incentives, combined with a flood of advertising from financial institutions, led four million people to opt out of SERPS by April 1990. Those taking out a personal pension received a rebate of 2 per cent on their national insurance contributions, and the cost of this to the government in terms of revenue foregone was estimated at £5.9 billion in 1990.[8] This, of course, was in addition to existing tax reliefs, and Richard Parry has calculated that during the 1980s total 'tax expenditures' on pensions rose from £2.6 billion to £6.5 billion, or from the equivalent of 15 per cent of direct public expenditure on pensions to 32 per cent.[9] The final value of the personal pensions taken out depends upon investment performance, and the increasing importance of private pensions means that the living standards of a growing proportion of retired people will depend less on political decisions regarding the level of benefits and more on the behaviour of the financial markets.

The restraint of public spending

There was nothing new in a Conservative government taking office with a commitment to restricting the overall level of public expenditure while increasing spending on specific areas such as defence and the police. What distinguished the Thatcher governments was the zeal with which they pursued these goals as they sought first to reduce and then to eliminate public sector borrowing. Without doubt the Budget of March 1981 was the watershed. Confronted with a severe and worsening recession, the Chancellor, Sir Geoffrey Howe, responded with what his best-known adviser called 'the biggest fiscal squeeze of peace time'.[10] Large increases were made in both direct and indirect taxes in order to reduce borrowing in accordance with the government's Medium Term Financial Strategy. In such a context, the pressures to reduce spending were immense. Moreover, social security was bound to be a prime target for cuts. Not only did it account for over one-third of all expenditure, but its alleged effects in terms of work incentives and the generation of 'dependency' were to attract increasing attention.

The 'ideological offensive' - benefits and dependency

The overriding importance attached to wealth creation meant that the chief themes of social security policy followed directly from the government's economic objectives – more targeting (ie, means-testing) to reduce expenditure and costs; more private provision to foster the 'enterprise culture'; 'simplification' to reduce civil servant numbers; more controls on benefit to deter abuse and reinforce work incentives. The Social Security Act 1986 embodied many of these themes. Nonetheless, the Act was also notable for what it did not do. SERPS was restricted but not abolished, while, most importantly, child benefit remained a universal benefit. It was this which led Nicholas Deakin to note the 'government's apparent abandonment near the end of its second term of office of its project of radical reform of welfare'.[11]

Mr Murray and Mr Moore

The election victory of 1987, however, brought a sharp change of mood and pace. The notorious tax-cutting Budget of 1988 was accompanied by radical legislation in education and housing and, of course, by the poll tax. Howard Glennerster and his colleagues have argued that, taken together, these constitute 'the most significant break in the incrementalist tradition in social policy' since 1948.[12] A similar pattern was evident in social security, as Ruth Lister notes:

In the third term, John Moore did not waste much time in signalling a much more aggressive ideological stance, making clear that the Social Security Act 1986 marked the beginning not the end of the process of reform.[13]

Central to this new aggressive stance were ideas about dependency, a 'benefits culture', and the *obligations* rather than the *rights* of claimants. In all this the government – and especially John Moore – were heavily influenced by the New Right thinking which had emerged in the United States.

In 1984, Charles Murray published *Losing Ground*, a brilliantly-written polemic which argued, in effect, that welfare programmes in the US had created rather than relieved poverty. 'I begin with the proposition', wrote Murray, 'that all, poor and non-poor alike, use the same general calculus in arriving at decisions.' The timescale, however, was different. 'Poor people play with fewer chips and cannot wait as long for results.' As a result, the 'behaviours that are "rational" are different at different economic levels'.[14]

Murray's crucial point was that the benefit system in the US gave poor people incentives to behave in ways that were against their long-term interests. The chief culprit was the Aid to Families with Dependent Children programme (AFDC), which provided cash assistance to low-income families. He argued that increases in the level of such payments, together with the liberalisation of the rules governing their receipt, made it rational for young women to opt for lone parenthood rather than low-paid work. Similarly, the acceptance of structural explanations of poverty led to an emphasis upon welfare rights and a refusal to discriminate between the deserving and the undeserving. This had eroded status relationships within poor communities, and destroyed work incentives:

> Because the system is to blame, all people on welfare are equally deserving... No one could disqualify himself on moral grounds from eligibility for public assistance – whether or not he was ready to help himself.[15]

Murray's book had a prodigious impact and gave rise to an exhaustive debate. It soon became clear that much of the data he used to support his case was unsound to say the least – especially the alleged link between the increase in one-parent families and the growth of AFDC payments. In part because of this, the New Right in the USA began to talk less of the 'rationality' of the poor, and more about the way in which the welfare system had so influenced the perceptions of the young as to create a 'dependency culture'. It was this aspect of the debate in the USA which John Moore seized upon.

In a speech in September 1987, Moore claimed that under 'the guise of compassion' people were encouraged to see themselves as 'victims of circumstance, mere putty in the grip of giant forces':

> Thus their confidence and will to help themselves was subtly undermined, and they were taught to think only government action could affect their lives... This kind of climate can in time corrupt the human spirit. Everyone knows the sullen apathy of dependence and can compare it with the sheer delight of human achievement.[16]

In the following year he must have dipped into *Losing Ground* again, to tell the Institute of Directors that:

> ...we were not sufficiently clear and explicit about the human qualities that as a society we admire and respect: qualities like effort, hard work, initiative and self respect. [Because of this] ... we have sent confusing messages that have undoubtedly contributed to the creation of a dependency culture. In a dependency culture people act in bizarre ways, because they are responding to perverse incentives.[17]

Examples of such perverse incentives included the poverty trap which discouraged people from seeking a better job or promotion; the old housing benefit scheme which provided more help to unemployed people than to those in work; and, of course, the fact that a young woman could jump the housing queue by becoming pregnant.

Moore's later speeches, however, also showed the influence of a second book which had been widely discussed in the United States – Lawrence Mead's *Beyond Entitlement*. Where Murray was concerned about incentives, Mead focused on obligations. Where Murray reformulated the Poor Law Report of 1833, Mead echoed Beatrice Webb's insistence that benefits be used to improve the behaviour of those who receive them. For Mead, the solution was not to abolish welfare, as Murray suggested, but to make it more authoritarian:

> The damage seems to be done, not by benefits by themselves, but by the fact that they were entitlements, given regardless of the behaviour of clients.[18]

The way to integrate the poor more effectively into the mainstream of society, then, was to make them work. The 'defining obligation' of citizenship was being willing to work in available jobs.[19]

Again, Mead's book was widely debated in the US where, as Ellwood notes, 'the notion of mutual responsibility is not controversial any more'. Nonetheless, the US experience demonstrates that, for it to be legitimate to require people to undertake work or training, the programmes themselves have to be worthwhile. 'There is not a shred of evidence to justify the claim that imposed work changes attitudes and expectations for the better.'[20]

It is often assumed in Britain that US provision is dominated by so-called workfare, under which claimants are required to work in return for benefits. However, as Louie Burghes and Robert Walker have shown, this is only a small part of US work/welfare schemes. Indeed, it is likely that it is Britain which has gone further in laying certain obligations on those people receiving benefits.[21]

In 1988, John Moore told the Conservative Party Conference that the government intended to correct 'the balance of the citizenship equation ... the equation that has "rights" on one side must have "responsibilities" on the other'.[22] This was not empty rhetoric. The Social Security Act 1989 required those claiming unemployment benefit, and income support when unemployed, to provide evidence that they were 'actively seeking work'. In Committee, Ministers emphasised that the test would be an 'objective' examination of the claimant's efforts. They also acknowledged, however, that it would be impossible for officials to check the accuracy of the statements made, and so the issue would effectively be one of whether or not they were prepared to believe individual claimants. As such, the new test appeared to differ little from the discredited 'genuinely seeking work' test of the 1920s.[23]

In the Commons, John Moore had argued that there was growing evidence that vacancies remained unfilled because the unemployed were not prepared to take them. It was quite wrong, he said, for such people to draw benefits 'at the expense of working people paying contributions and taxes. Nor is it doing any service to claimants or their families to allow them to drop out of the world of work when so many vacancies are available.'[24]

The Act also reduced to thirteen weeks the length of time that a claimant could hold out for employment on terms and conditions similar to her or his last job, while the penalty for leaving a job voluntarily had already been increased substantially, and the right to income support had been withdrawn from most 16- to 17-year-olds.[25]

The nature of dependency

The emphasis upon dependency raises issues far wider than that of unemployment benefit. As many have pointed out, the government was effectively transferring rather than reducing dependency. This transfer took two principal forms.

First, it was seeking to make people less dependent upon the state and more dependent upon voluntary bodies. Indeed, another feature of these years was the growth in Conservative rhetoric regarding the role and responsibilities of the 'active citizen'. It should be noted that, however uplifting voluntary work may be for the new model citizen, in the field of income maintenance charity is experienced by its recipients as *more* stigmatising and *less* dependable than state welfare. More generally, it has been argued that an emphasis upon market values is likely to corrode rather than foster feelings of altruism.[26]

Second, the government was trying to reduce the public dependency of women upon the state, and to reinforce their private dependency on men. Ruth Lister has shown how the financial independence of women was eroded in the 1980s, and how the philosophy of self-reliance was not extended to women's 'natural economic dependency' within the household.[27] (Chapter 3 outlines the extent to which women have borne the brunt of the hardships generated by the benefit changes.) One consequence of this patriarchal view of dependency was that discussion of work incentives referred almost entirely to men. This was in sharp contrast to the United States, where the dependency debate was preoccupied with the effects of AFDC payments upon the labour force participation of lone mothers.

In Britain, official pronouncements on lone mothers were ambiguous. It was not clear whether they were expected to remain at home and care for their children, in which case they would need an adequate income, or to seek work, in which case they would need adequate provision for childcare. The stock answer was that the government wanted to give them a choice, though in practice this was between work without childcare support, or caring on a low income.

One aspect which did prompt action in Whitehall was the growing burden on the public purse which arose from the failure of many absent parents, usually fathers, to contribute to the maintenance of their children. In October 1990, the White Paper, 'Children Come First', proposed a new machinery for the payment of maintenance.[28]

The principle of requiring fathers to meet their obligations received widespread support, but critics pointed out that relatively little of the money would go to the children. Nonetheless, the White Paper did not seek to worsen the circumstances of lone mothers (unless they refused to identify the father 'without good cause'). To that extent it departed from the position of those such as Murray who had argued, in effect, that the problem could only be reduced by making lone parenthood less attractive. By 1990, however, the 'neo-liberal hour' appeared to have past.

Losing momentum?

The implementation of Thatcherism had often been opposed by interest groups. Small businesses, in particular, had resented being asked to administer statutory sick pay, and had resisted the payment of family credit through the pay-packet. Industry in general had opposed the abolition of SERPS, and Conservative women's organisations had lobbied powerfully in defence of child benefit. There were no such powerful groups to defend unemployed people and lone parents, who were most at risk from a campaign against the 'benefits culture'. Nonetheless, that campaign also appeared to wane during 1990, as the government seemed once more to lose its appetite for radical reform.

Current Conservative policies are considered in Chapter 8. Suffice it to note here that the election of John Major – and the earlier replacement of John Moore by Tony Newton – have been followed by a marked change of emphasis. For example, Tony Newton's speech to the 1990 Conservative Party Conference made no mention of benefit 'dependency' and proclaimed as an achievement the spending on social security which his predecessor had sought so obviously to cut. But the clearest indication of a change in direction was the decision in the 1991 Budget to index the value of child benefit.

The most important reason for this more cautious approach was the perceived decline in popular support for radical change. There had always been a 'triumphalist' element in Thatcherism, a belief that the government was setting the people free and that the people would be grateful. Although this conviction was consistently challenged by poll evidence, which showed continued support for spending on the social services and the welfare state (see Chapter 4), this problem seemed to be outweighed by the 'two-thirds/one-third' strategy cited earlier, and by the fact that general elections were decided on other issues. It was the fiasco of the poll tax that brought problems of a quite different order.

One of the main objectives of the poll tax was to curb local authority spending. This was to be achieved by ensuring that the cost of providing services was borne by a far higher proportion of the electorate, and by structuring central grants in such a way that any increase in an authority's spending had a disproportionate impact upon the level of the poll tax it was required to set. In the event, however, the government's disregard of distributional issues and its arrogant dismissal of criticism led it to decide upon a regressive and deeply unpopular flat-rate charge. The public hostility this engendered allowed the local authorities to increase their spending in the knowledge that the voters would blame the government. The result was an unprecedented retreat and loss of confidence within the government which was then compounded by the equally hostile reception of its reforms in the National Health Service.

Welcome as all this may have been to Thatcherism's critics and victims, it is important not to exaggerate the change which has occurred. The four central themes outlined at the start of this chapter – the acceptance of inequalities, the repudiation of government responsibility for unemployment, privatisation, and, the restraint of public spending – all remain, as was illustrated by Chancellor Norman Lamont's callous remark in the Commons that unemployment was 'a price well worth paying' for lower inflation.[29] The question as to *who* paid the price of Thatcherism is considered in the next chapter.

Notes

1. A Gamble, 'Thatcherism and Conservative politics', in S Hall and M Jacques (eds), *The Politics of Thatcherism,* Lawrence and Wishart, 1983, p114.
2. C Oppenheim, *Poverty: The Facts,* CPAG Ltd, 1990.
3. Speech to Greater London Conservative Political Centre, 11 May 1989.
4. Sir Keith Joseph, *Conditions for Fuller Employment,* Centre for Policy Studies, 1978, p20.
5. A Walker, 'The strategy of inequality', in I Taylor (ed), *The Social Effects of Free Market Policies,* Harvester Wheatsheaf, 1990, p44.
6. Compare with J Lawlor, 'Monthly unemployment statistics: maintaining a consistent series', *Employment Gazette,* December 1990.
7. Speech, Conservative Party Conference, 12 October 1988.

8.   National Audit Office, *The Elderly: Information Requirements for Supporting the Elderly and Implications of Personal Pensions for the National Insurance Fund,* HMSO, 1991, p18.

9.   R Parry, 'The privatisation of welfare under the Thatcher government', in *Business in the Contemporary World,* Spring 1991.

10. Sir Alan Walters, quoted in M Holmes, *The First Thatcher Government 1979-1983,* Wheatsheaf, 1985, p61.

11. N Deakin, *The Politics of Welfare,* Methuen, 1987, p165.

12. H Glennerster, A Powers and T Travers, 'A new era for social policy: a new enlightenment or a new leviathian?', *Journal of Social Policy,* Vol 20, No 3, 1991.

13. R Lister, 'Social security in the 1980s', *Social Policy and Administration,* Vol 25, No 2, 1991.

14. C Murray, *Losing Ground,* Basic Books, 1984, p155.

15. *See* note 14, p182.

16. Speech to Conservative Political Centre, 26 September 1987. At this point in time John Moore was Secretary of State for Social Services. In the Autumn of 1988 he became Secretary of State for Social Security.

17. Lecture to Institute of Directors, 8 June 1988.

18. L Mead, *Beyond Entitlement,* Free Press, 1986, p65.

19. *See* note 18, p230.

20. D Ellwood, *Poor Support,* Basic Books, 1988, p228.

21. R Walker, *Thinking about Workfare: Evidence from the USA,* HMSO, 1991.

22. Speech to Conservative Party Conference, 12 October 1988.

23. A Deacon, 'Back to the twenties for the unemployed', in *Community Care,* 9 February 1989.

24. *Hansard,* 10 January 1989, col 717.

25. The extent to which these and other measures increased the effective job search of claimants is a technical and contentious area. See, for example, J Philpott, *A Solution to Long-Term Unemployment: The Job Guarantee,* Employment Institute, 1990.

26. A Ware, 'Meeting needs through voluntary action. Does market society corrode altruism?', in A Ware and R Goodin (eds), *Needs and Welfare,* Sage, 1990.

27. R Lister, 'Women, economic dependency and citizenship', in *Journal of Social Policy,* Vol 19, No 4, 1990.

28. Cmnd 1264, HMSO, 1990.

29. *Hansard,* 16 May 1991, col 413.

3.
Bearing the cost

Jane Millar

IN the 1980s, social policy was to a large extent determined by the demands of economic policy. The previous chapter argued that at the heart of government policy during these years was the ideology of the market, with its constant pressure to control and reduce public expenditure, with its policies of privatisation and deregulation, and with the introduction of quasi-markets in welfare services. The impacts and effects of these policies are far from neutral. Some individuals and groups have borne a greater burden that others may benefit. This chapter sets out to identify what has been happening to the incomes and living standards of poor people over the past decade. It is people in poverty who have often borne the heaviest cost of the Thatcher years.

Inequality and poverty in the 1980s

Throughout this century up until the 1980s British society had been becoming less unequal. The process had been slow – in 1930 the top 5 per cent of the population owned 79 per cent of total personal wealth; by 1950 this had fallen to 74 per cent, by 1960 to 59 per cent and by 1970 to 54 per cent.[1] But in the 1980s this long-term trend to greater equality apparently came to a halt, and was perhaps even reversed. In relation to both wealth (which includes the value of assets such as housing and pension rights) and income (which comes mainly from earnings), the gap between top and bottom has been widening.

Inland Revenue statistics on wealth holdings show that the total marketable wealth of the top 5 per cent was 38 per cent in 1976, down to 36 per cent in 1981, but back up to 38 per cent in 1988. The wealth of the bottom half of the population has always been negligible – in 1976 and 1981 it amounted to about 8 per cent of the total, falling to only 6 per cent in 1988.[2] Between 1980 and 1989, the

value of company share prices almost quadrupled, to the benefit
almost exclusively of the very wealthy.[3]
    Income inequality has also increased significantly in the 1980s.
The 1988 *Households Below Average Income* statistics[4] showed that
between 1979 and 1988:

- the poorest tenth of the population had an increase of only 2 per
  cent in their real disposable income (adjusted for household
  size) after paying their housing costs;
- the average had an increase of 33.5 per cent in real disposable
  income.

Households Below Average Income only shows incomes up to the
average; the higher income groups must, however, have had much
larger increases in real income between 1979 and 1988 for the
average increase to be 33.5 per cent.
    Of course, those who make up the bottom 10 per cent were not
the same people in 1979 and 1988. The people will have changed;
but, as the figures show, there was a widening gap over the 1980s
even between the bottom 10 per cent and the average, leaving aside
the better-off. The poorest were therefore worse off relative to other
groups.
    However, this increase in income inequality does not necessarily
mean that there has been an increase in poverty, since those at the
bottom of the income distribution could still have incomes adequate
for their needs, even if they have become worse off compared with the
rest of society. In the 1980s, the questions of how poverty should be
defined and measured, and how to determine the extent of poverty,
became simultaneously highly political and highly technical.[5] Here,
two different sorts of measures will be used to show the extent of
poverty in Britain in the 1980s:[6] the official statistics on households
with incomes of less than half the average (the 'income poverty line');
and the evidence from the two *Breadline Britain* surveys on the
number of households lacking basic necessities (the 'basic essentials
poverty line').[7] These present two contrasting approaches to the
measurement of poverty, but a consistent picture of the trends.

'Income poverty line'

Official government statistics detail the number of households with
'below average income'. This implies no clear and objective 'poverty

line', but taking households with below half the average income, after meeting housing costs, gives an indication of the number and type of the poorest households.[8] Income is adjusted ('equivalised') for household size and in 1990 half the average would have been about £52 per week for a single person and £134 for a couple with two children aged three and six. Table 1 shows the increase in the number and proportion of individuals living in poor households, by this measure, during the 1980s. In 1979 there were almost 5 million people in poverty, or about 9 per cent of the population. By 1988 this had risen to 11.75 million, almost 22 per cent of the population.

TABLE 1
Poverty in the 1980s: 'Income poverty line'
Less than 50 per cent of average equivalent income,
after housing costs

	Number of persons (millions)	Proportion (%)
1979	4.9	9.4
1981	6.4	11.9
1983	6.2	11.5
1985	7.2	13.4
1987	10.5	19.4
1988	11.8	21.6

Figures rounded to nearest 100,000.
SOURCE: *Low Income Statistics*, Table F2.[9]

'Basic essentials poverty line'

In the two *Breadline Britain* surveys of 1983 and 1990, a person is defined as poor if they live in a household that cannot afford three or more basic necessities – items such as hot meals, heating and non-damp accommodation (see also Chapter 4). These 'basic necessities' are derived from survey data on what people in general think should be considered essential. Thus, this measure of poverty is to a large extent shaped by popular thinking, since it is based on society's general views about what constitutes an acceptable standard of living. Table 2 shows the results. According to these figures, the number of poor people increased from about 7.5 million in 1983 to 11 million in 1990 – or from about 14 to about 20 per cent of the population. Severe poverty also increased substantially.

TABLE 2
Poverty in 1983 and 1990: 'Basic essentials poverty line'

	In poverty*		In severe poverty**	
	number of persons (millions)	proportion (%)	number of persons (millions)	proportion (%)
1983	7.5	14.0	2.6	4.8
1990	11.0	20.0	3.5	6.3

* unable to afford at least three essential items
** unable to afford at least seven essential items

SOURCE: Breadline Britain in the 1990s.[10]

The similarity between these estimates is striking – between *eleven and twelve million* people in Britain are living in, or very close to, poverty. This amounts to *one person in every five*. But even this figure will underestimate the actual extent of poverty because both these estimates are based on household data, which has two main problems. First, they do not count people living *outside* households – for example, the growing number of homeless people and those living in hostel accommodation. In 1989 there were estimated to be almost 0.7 million homeless people.[11] Second, household-based income estimates are insensitive to the distribution of income within households, and so will undercount poor people living in non-poor households. It is mainly women who are likely to be in this situation.[12]

Who is in poverty?

Pensioners' incomes have fallen relative to the average because the value of pensions has fallen behind average earnings (see below for further discussion). However, it is people of working age who make up the vast majority of 'heads' of low-income households. Of the 11.75 million people living in households with incomes below half the average (after meeting housing costs) in 1988:

- 3.5 million were in pensioner households;
- 2.6 million were in households with an unemployed head;
- 2.4 million were in households with a head in full-time work;
- 1.5 million were in households headed by a lone parent not in full-time work;
- 0.7 million were in households with a sick or disabled head;
- 1 million were in 'other' households - such as early retired men, widows, students, and so on.[13]

Children in poverty

The increase in poverty among people of working age means that children are also increasingly at risk of poverty. In 1979, about 1.6 million children lived in poor households; by 1988, this had risen to about 3 million children - 25 per cent of all children in Britain. Of these children, about 1 million were living in households where the head was in full-time work, and about 1.7 million were in households where the head was either unemployed (0.8 million), or a lone parent not in full-time work (0.9 million).[14]

Bradshaw has recently carried out a survey of the circumstances of British children on behalf of the United Nations Children's Fund (UNICEF). He points to the lack of adequate data on the circumstances of children in Britain, but also concludes that:

> During the 1980s children have borne the brunt of the changes that have occurred in the economic conditions, demographic structure and social policies of the UK... There is no evidence that improvements in the living standards of the better-off have 'trickled down' to low income families with children.[15]

Causes of poverty

The main reason why poverty has increased over the past decade is the growing numbers of people who can no longer obtain an adequate and secure income through employment. There are three main reasons for this situation.

First, the continuing high and persistent levels of unemployment. In mid-1991 there were about 2.2 million people officially registered as unemployed, another million or so who would have registered if the official definition had not changed, and perhaps another 2 million people who would have liked regular employment, although they were not at that time looking for work.[16]

The burden of unemployment is not equally shared. It falls most heavily in certain regions (eg, Northern Ireland, Scotland, the North and the North-West); on younger and older workers (under 20-year-olds and over 50-year-olds in particular); and on people from ethnic minorities, who can have unemployment rates twice or three times the rate for the white population. During the 1980s, the type of people most at risk of unemployment changed very little – those registering as unemployed were predominantly young, unskilled, low-paid workers, most of whom had been unemployed before.[17]

The second reason that poverty has been increasing is the rising incidence of low-paid work. In 1982, 3.5 million full-time workers were low paid (defined by the Low Pay Unit as less than two-thirds of median male earnings). By 1988, this number had risen to 5.6 million. In addition, more than 4 million part-time workers were also low paid. Most of these low-paid part-time workers were women. Women continue to constitute two-thirds of all low-paid workers.[18] Those with the lowest earnings have steadily fallen behind the average. In 1979, the earnings for men in the bottom 10 per cent of the earnings distribution were equivalent to about 66 per cent of median male earnings. By 1989, this had fallen to about 59 per cent.[19]

The third reason for increased poverty is the significant growth in 'precarious' or 'flexible' employment over recent years. This includes part-time work, self-employment, temporary or seasonal work and homeworking. In 1986, about one-third of the workforce, or around 8 million workers, were in precarious employment.[20] Women make up the vast majority of these workers, and much of the growth in employment in the 1980s was a consequence of married women taking up part-time employment. The impact of this increase in women's employment has been mixed. On the one hand, it has meant more financial independence for women in the family. It has also significantly reduced the risk of family poverty, not least because women's earnings are usually spent on the needs of the family as a whole.[21] On the other hand, in many families a single earner often cannot earn enough to keep her/his family out of poverty. Women's earnings are therefore essential, not optional, for these families. Increasingly, the 'family wage' means two low wages, both necessary to reach an adequate income level. Those families with no earners (as in many unemployed families) or with only one earner (lone parents and parents of very young children) are therefore particularly disadvantaged.

These three trends – higher unemployment, lower pay and more precarious employment – clearly relate to, and reinforce, one another. It is women who make up the vast majority of part-time and low-paid workers and it is men in unskilled and low-paid jobs who are most vulnerable to unemployment. Young people cannot get a secure hold in the labour market and instead move between unemployment, low-paid work, and low-paid training schemes, while older workers cannot get back into work if they lose their jobs. Again, as indicated earlier, black people face an even greater vulnerability to unemployment and low pay. Class, gender, race, age and where people live all interact to create disadvantage for some workers and advantage for others, and the increasing polarisation of the labour market which took place in the 1980s has become apparent not just in the UK but also in other industrialised countries.[22]

However, although these labour market trends are part of long-term employment restructuring, government policies during the 1980s have exacerbated their impact. The UK government's continuing opposition to the European Community's Charter of Fundamental Social Rights of Workers and to the draft directives on, for example, part-time work and parental leave, reflect its view that an unregulated labour market is most efficient. This view has also been reflected in domestic employment policy, sometimes exacerbating existing problems; and several policies, introduced during the 1980s in particular, directly affect women:

- Protective legislation applying to women's hours of work and conditions has been abolished, so that, for example, since 1988 there have been no restrictions on night-working for women.
- Since 1980 rights to reinstatement after maternity leave do not apply to those working for employers with fewer than six employees.
- Job loss is inadequately protected against for many part-time and low-paid workers. About two million workers in 1985-87 were not in the national insurance scheme because they had earnings below the 'lower earnings limit' and so were not entitled to national insurance benefits. Most of these people are married women who are rarely eligible for income support because of the family means test which takes into account their

husbands' earnings.
- The powers and rights of trade unions have been restricted.
- The wages of young workers are no longer protected by wages councils, and minimum wages are now set only for workers aged over 21 in certain industries.
- Most employment rights apply only to those who work more than sixteen hours per week and who have been with the same employer for at least two years; or for more than eight hours per week and with the same employer for more than five years. Thus, many part-time and temporary workers are excluded from any form of employment protection.[23]

Employment is increasingly unable to provide a secure and adequate income for many people. State protection for vulnerable workers has been reduced. These trends and policies represent a very fundamental challenge to the basis of the post-war social security system. The assumptions underlying that system – full employment and an adequate 'family' wage – seemingly no longer hold. For many people, there are no jobs and those that do exist are often low paid and insecure. Needs are changing and require different social security provisions to reflect the current situation. The next section of this chapter therefore examines the support offered by the social security system for those people who have been finding it increasingly difficult to support themselves through employment.

Social security and poverty

Throughout the 1980s social security provisions were subject to an almost constant barrage of reviews and revisions, often with the aim of regulating or controlling public expenditure. There were major Social Security Acts in 1980, 1982, 1986 and 1988, as well as numerous changes to regulations. One of the main thrusts of the changes has been the emphasis on targeting, and on using means tests to direct resources to those people 'most in need'. However, from the point of view of people who are reliant on state social security support, the overall result has been a system which, for many claimants, provides lower benefits, which are less reliable and harder to access.[24]

Lower benefits

For a government dedicated to the cutting back of public expenditure, social security – as the largest single item of expenditure – clearly could not be ignored. Barr and Coulter have recently carried out a detailed analysis of social security expenditure from the early 1970s to the late 1980s.[25] Overall spending has increased in real terms – up from about £33.6 billion (at 1987/88 prices) in 1979/80 to about £43.2 billion in 1988/89. However, in the 1980s most of the increase in expenditure was a consequence of increased numbers of recipients: especially more unemployed people, but also more lone parents, more pensioners and more claimants with disabilities. Only about a third of the increase can be attributed to increased benefit levels.

In particular, benefits for unemployed people fell in real terms over the 1980s. Atkinson and Micklewright estimated that if the 1979 benefits system had been in place in 1988, an extra £510 million would have been spent on unemployed people.[26] This would have meant each person receiving an extra £3.21 per week on average. As a result of the breaking of the link between pensions and earnings in 1980, pensioners have also lost out. Since then, pensions have risen only in line with prices, and by 1987 a single pensioner was £7.15 per week worse off, and a pensioner couple £11.30 per week worse off, than they would have been had the link with earnings been maintained. Housing benefit was cut by about £900 million in the 1980s.[27] Child benefit was frozen between 1988 and 1990, although there was an increase of £1 per week for the first or eldest eligible child only from April 1991 and the 1991 Budget did announce a further increase from October 1991 of £1 for the first or eldest eligible child and 25 pence for subsequent children, with a commitment to index-link the benefit from April 1992. Over 80 per cent of couples with children and about 74 per cent of lone-parent families lost out financially overall when income support replaced supplementary benefit.[28]

Townsend has recently estimated that as much as £7-8 billion more would have been spent on social security benefits in 1989 if benefit structures and provisions for upratings had been the same as in 1979.[29] Hills, looking at tax and social security changes between 1979 and 1988, concludes that:

> The cuts in direct taxes have been entirely paid for by cuts in the generosity of benefits ... there has been a major redistribution from those on low incomes to the better-off.[30]

Restricted access

Access to social security support has been restricted for several groups, especially for young and unemployed people. Young people aged 16 and 17 are no longer entitled to income support, except in certain limited circumstances, as it is assumed that they will be in paid employment or on a training scheme. Unemployed people have to satisfy more stringent tests to prove they are not 'voluntarily unemployed', and that they are available for and 'actively seeking' work. Disqualification from unemployment benefit for voluntary unemployment has been increased from six weeks to six months. The introduction of statutory sick pay and statutory maternity pay, administered and partly paid for by employers, has made it more difficult for some workers to receive these benefits.[31] Black claimants are increasingly asked to prove residence and to show passports, and some people can only enter the UK if they can prove that they can be supported without recourse to 'public funds',[32] which, in effect, means giving up their right to income support and other benefits. This is an issue which is returned to in Chapter 7.

Less reliable support

The increased role played by means-tested benefits means that claimants can no longer be assured of receiving support. Child benefit, with a take-up rate of almost 100 per cent, was frozen for three years, while some increases were made in family credit, which has a take-up rate of about half of those eligible, and is payable for only six months before a new claim has to be made. Housing costs are not met in full for those on income support – all claimants have to pay 20 per cent of their poll tax, and only 50 per cent of mortgage interest repayments are met during the first sixteen weeks on income support. Additionally, income support can be reduced to pay back social fund loans and for poll tax, rent, gas, water or electricity arrears – a list which appears to be growing all the time.[33] Thus, many people now have incomes well below the 'safety net'.

The discretionary social fund

These three features – reduced benefits, restricted access, and less reliability – are all embodied within the discretion-based part of the social fund. Introduced in 1988, the social fund replaced the former system of single payments and urgent needs payments with interest-free loans for most claimants (though grants remain available in certain circumstances). The gross budget for the discretionary social fund in 1989/90 was £203 million, compared with expenditure of £335 million for single payments in 1985-86. Those who have been on income support for less than six months are not eligible to apply for budgeting loans, and claimants not in 'priority groups' rarely receive loans – or community care grants for that matter. Claimants are likely to be refused a loan if it is considered that they cannot meet the repayments. As a result, those in most need of payments rarely receive extra help. Social fund loans and grants are made at the discretion of benefit officers and are subject to a budget which is cash-limited. Two-parent families with children lose out particularly as a consequence of the discretionary social fund.[34]

Living in poverty

The consequences of poverty are often hidden from public view, especially in families with children, where mothers in particular bear the cost of the day-to-day managing of, and coping with, poverty. Studies of the living standards of those on benefits show that these poor families are able to survive only at great personal cost – cutting back on essentials, being unable to afford an adequate diet, often worrying about money and falling into debt.[35] For children, there are likely to be long-term effects – Bradshaw notes that high infant mortality, low birth weight, preventable causes of childhood death, rates of disability, rates of dental decay, low growth rates and poor nutrition are all associated with poverty amongst children.[36]

Although much of this family poverty remains out of sight, one of its more visible consequences has been the rapid rise in homelessness and the number of people now sleeping rough in the streets of Britain's major cities. Young people, without access to social security and often without a family who can (or want to) help, are particularly at risk. Shelter estimates that over 150,000 young people experience homelessness every year, and in 1989 there were estimated to be between 121,000 and 125,000 single homeless people in London alone.[37]

While some people cannot get access to housing, others are finding themselves at risk of losing their home. The proportion of homes which are owner-occupied has risen from 52 per cent in 1979 to 64 per cent in 1988,[38] partly as a consequence of government policy to cut back on house-building and to sell existing local authority housing stock. The spread of owner occupation has given some people access to a valuable asset for the first time but, like the rise in two-earner families, this is something of a mixed blessing. Housing costs have been rising very substantially, and repossessions by building societies increased from 4,000 in 1981, to 14,000 in 1989.[39] In 1988, 135,000 households were accepted as homeless by local authorities. Over two-thirds of these were families with children, because homeless people without children receive little statutory help.[40]

Conclusion

This chapter has concentrated on poverty and shown how this increased substantially in the 1980s. The main causes of this increase are to be found in the labour market, and in the fact that growing numbers of people cannot get access to secure employment with adequate wages. However, rather than providing protection against these changes, government policy has exacerbated their effects. Unemployment, a deregulated labour market, lower social security benefits – which are harder to access, and less reliable when they are received – have all contributed to the rise of poverty and insecurity. And while poverty has been rising, government attitudes towards poor people have hardened, with people in poverty often being blamed for their situations – 'unemployed people do not want to work', 'lone parents are irresponsible', 'young people expect too much', and so on. As the previous chapter demonstrated, the problem of poverty has increasingly been defined as a problem of a 'dependency culture', and not as a consequence of recent economic and social policy.

Increased poverty is a reflection of growing divisions in our society – which has become more unequal not just in income and wealth, but also more generally in the resources people can get access to, and the quality of life they can obtain. It has been suggested [41] that the social security system in the 1980s was actually very successful in coping with economic restructuring, maintaining minimum incomes and coping with high levels of unemployment without this leading to mass social unrest and disorder. But even if this is true, some people have borne the cost of this economic change while others have reaped the benefits. Inequality has increased and poverty has once again become a common experience for many people.

Notes

1. A B Atkinson, *The Economics of Inequality*, Clarendon Press, 1983 (2nd edition).
2. Central Statistical Office, *Social Trends 1991*, HMSO, 1991.
3. T Stark, *Income and Wealth in the 1980s*, Fabian Society, 1990.
4. *Low Income Statistics: Households Below Average Income: Tables 1988*, Social Security Committee, First Report, Session 1990-91, Cmnd 401, HMSO, 1991, Table D1. Commissioned from IFS by the Social Security Committee.
5. See, for example,*The Journal of Social Policy*, Vol 16, Part 2; C Glendinning and J Millar (eds), *Women and Poverty in Britain*, Wheatsheaf, 1987; P Johnson and S Webb, *Poverty in Official Statistics*, IFS, 1990; C Oppenheim, *Poverty: The Facts*, CPAG Ltd, 1990.
6. These figures refer to Great Britain and not to the United Kingdom as a whole. They thus exclude Northern Ireland, where receipt of benefits, low pay and poverty are all more prevalent than they are in the rest of the country. See, for example, E Evason, *On the Edge*, CPAG Ltd, 1985.
7. J Mack and S Lansley, *Poor Britain*, Unwin, 1985; H Frayman, *Breadline Britain in the 1990s*, Domino Films/LWT, 1991.
8. The published tables give details of income before and after housing costs. Income after housing costs, as presented here, is a more reliable guide to living standards given that, for many people, housing represents a fixed cost. See Johnson and Webb, note 5 above, for further discussion. A poverty line set at 50 per cent of average income has also been used in a recent European Commission sponsored study by M O'Higgins and S Jenkins, *Poverty in Europe, 1975, 1980 and 1985*, paper presented at EC Seminar on Poverty Statistics, the Netherlands, 1989. An update of this work uses half of average expenditure rather than income; see P Johnson and S Webb, *UK Poverty Statistics: A Comparative Study*, IFS, 1991.
9. Social Security Committee, *Low Income Statistics: Households Below Average Income: Tables 1988*, HMSO, 1991.
10. *See* note 7.
11. The number of households accepted as homeless rose from about 53,000 in 1978 to about 140,000 in 1989; and the number of households in temporary accommodation rose from about 10,000 in 1976 to about 36,000 in 1989. See J Greve and E Currie, *Homelessness in Britain*, JRMT, 1990; A Murie, *Housing Inequality and Deprivation,* Heinemann, 1983.
12. J Millar and C Glendinning, 'Gender and poverty', *Journal of Social Policy*, Vol 18, No 3, 1989.

13.   *See* note 9.

14.   *See* note 9. (Poverty defined as below half average income.)

15.   J Bradshaw, *Child Poverty and Deprivation in the UK*, National Children's Bureau, 1990.

16.   Department of Employment, *Employment Gazette*, May 1991; Unemployment Unit/Youthaid, *Working Brief*, May 1991; NEDO, *Defusing the Demographic Time-bomb*, HMSO, 1989.

17.   In 1987-89, the average unemployment rate for white people was about 9 per cent compared with 16 per cent for West Indian/Guyanese people; 11 per cent for Indian people; and 25 per cent for Pakistani/Bangladeshi people: Department of Employment, *Employment Gazette*, February 1991. See also B Erens and B Hedges, *Survey of Incomes In and Out of Work*, SCPR, 1990; and S Moylan, J Millar and B Davies, *For Richer, for Poorer*, HMSO, 1987.

18.   Low Pay Unit, *Low Pay in Britain and the Regions*, Low Pay Unit Parliamentary Briefing No 1, 1990.

19.   H Parker, *Basic Income and the Labour Market*, Basic Income Research Group, 1991.

20.   Of these, 5.1 million were part-time workers, 2.7 million were self-employed and 1.6 million were temporary workers: U Huws, J Hurstfield and R Holtmatt, *What Price Flexibility?*, Low Pay Unit, 1989.

21.   J Pahl, *Money and Marriage*, Macmillan, 1989; J Millar, 'Mothers, employment and poverty', in R Davidson and A Erskine (eds), *Poverty and Deprivation*, Jessica Kingsley, 1991.

22.   See, for example, G Rodgers and J Rodgers, *Precarious Jobs*, ILO, 1989; and Commission of the European Communities, *Employment in Europe*, EC, 1990.

23.   C Glendinning, 'Impoverishing women', in A Walker and C Walker (eds), *The Growing Divide*, CPAG Ltd, 1987; J Lewis and C Davies, 'Protective legislation in Britain, 1870-1990', *Policy and Politics*, Vol 19, No 1, 1991; C Hakim, 'Work force re-structuring, social insurance coverage and the black economy', *Journal of Social Policy*, Vol 18, No 4, 1989; S McRae and W W Daniel, *Maternity Rights: First Findings*, PSI, 1991.

24.   *See* A Walker and C Walker (eds), note 23; R Lister, 'Social security in the 1980s', *Social Policy and Administration*, Vol 25, No 2, 1991.

25.   N Barr and F Coulter, 'Social security: problem or solution?', in J Hills (ed), *The State of Welfare*, Clarendon Press, 1990.

26.   A B Atkinson and J Micklewright, 'Turning the screw: benefits for the unemployed, 1979-1988', in A B Atkinson, *Poverty and Social Security*, Harvester Wheatsheaf, 1989.

27.   R Lister, 'Social security', in M McCarthy (ed), *The New Politics of Welfare*, Macmillan, 1989. See also P Alcock, 'The end of the line for social security: the Thatcherite restructuring of welfare', *Critical Social Policy*, Vol 30, 1990/91.

28.   M Svenson and S MacPherson, 'Real losses and unreal figures: the impact of the 1986 Social Security Act', in S Becker and S MacPherson (eds), *Public Issues, Private Pain*, Insight, 1988.

29.   P Townsend, *The Poor are Poorer: A Statistical Report on Changes in the Living Standards of Rich and Poor in the UK 1979-1989*, Bristol University, 1991.

30.   J Hills, *Changing Tax*, CPAG Ltd, 1988, p13. This assumes a situation where benefits would have been increased in line with the growth in national income.
31.   S Baloo, I McMaster and K Sutton, *Statutory Sick Pay: The Failure of Privatisation in Social Security*, Leicester City Council, 1986; House of Commons Committee of Public Accounts, *Statutory Sick Pay*, HMSO, 1985; S McRae and W W Daniel, *see* note 23.
32.   C Oppenheim, *see* note 5.
33.   In 1989 there were about 130,000 income support recipients with deductions for electricity, 134,000 with deductions for gas, 51,000 with reductions for rent arrears and 352,000 repaying social fund loans: C Oppenheim, *see* note 5. There are also plans to allow deductions from income support for child support and for fines.
34.   See S Becker and R Silburn, *The New Poor Clients*, Community Care/Benefits Research Unit, 1990; Social Security Research Consortium, *Cash Limited, Limited Cash*, AMA, 1991; National Audit Office, *The Social Fund*, HMSO, 1991.
35.   P Heady and M Smyth, *Living Standards during Unemployment*, OPCS, 1989; J Bradshaw and H Holmes, *Living on the Edge*, Tyneside CPAG, 1989; S Payne, *Women, Health and Poverty*, Harvester Wheatsheaf, 1991; H Graham, 'Caring in poverty: women in low-income households', in C Glendinning and J Millar (eds), *Women and Poverty in Britain*, (2nd edition), Harvester Wheatsheaf, 1991; J Bradshaw and J Millar, *Lone-parent Families in the UK*, HMSO, 1991.
36.   *See* note 15.
37.   *See* note 15.
38.   OPCS, *General Household Survey 1988*, HMSO, 1990.
39.   R Berthoud, *Credit, Debt and Poverty*, HMSO, 1989.
40.   *See* note 2.
41.   H Glennerster, 'What commitment to welfare?', 1988, cited in J LeGrand, *The State of Welfare*, in J Hills (ed), *see* note 25.

Acknowledgement

Thanks to Stephen Jenkins, Tim Lee and readers for their comments and suggestions.

4.
Poor attitudes

Peter Golding

MOVING the debate about poverty on through the 1990s will require more than brain-storming within the poverty lobby. As always, it will rest on the ability to build up public support for what may be radical new perceptions and solutions. How people construe poverty, their attitudes, prejudices, and beliefs, are significant for two fundamental reasons. First, they set the limits to what is politically feasible. What people know and believe about benefit levels or the circumstances of claimants and low-paid people, not to mention their broader visions of social inequality, will form the framework within which they can be persuaded of the virtue or otherwise of redistributive policies in aid of poorer groups. Second, as the gap widens between comfortable Britain and those increasingly isolated from late twentieth century affluence, direct experience is increasingly replaced by prejudice. Both geographical and social divides make the observation of poverty a remote prospect for many of Britain's more affluent majority. The occasional embarrassment of a supplicant hand by the underground station entrance or uncomfortable images on a late night documentary become, for a significant majority, but intermittent interruptions in a life of contented distance from Britain's poor.

This chapter reviews changes in public opinion through the 1980s, drawing on some of the major social surveys conducted during the decade. It also reflects on the lessons to be drawn for both policy and campaigning on a new agenda in the 1990s.

Poverty perceived: the public mood in the 1980s

Attitude surveys are not necessarily the best, and certainly not the only, means for reading shifts in public values and beliefs. However, there have been a number of studies which have addressed the question of attitudes to poverty. What follows is primarily based on such work.[1]

Certainly poverty has not been totally invisible. The majority of the public accepts that poverty does exist in Britain. In 1983, 55 per cent agreed that there was 'such a thing as real poverty in Britain today', while by 1989, 63 per cent agreed with the view that 'there is quite a lot of real poverty in Britain today'. Nonetheless, this is not much of a shift, given the substantial rise in the numbers living in poverty in these years (see Chapter 3 for a full discussion). And within this majority lies a number of dissenting minorities. In 1983, pensioners, the self-employed and Conservative voters were far less likely to agree with this view than people with children or unemployed people. By 1986, the political divide had sharpened – 59 per cent of Conservative voters thought there was 'very little poverty in Britain today', compared with 27 per cent of Labour voters.[2]

Of course, such sweeping judgements rest on some assessment of what poverty actually means to these different groups. While academics and civil servants tussle over the minutiae of the statistics, and occasionally mount a grand confrontation over the definition of the term, public views of poverty appear irretrievably basic. Table 1 shows the response to an invitation to consider three definitions of poverty.

TABLE 1
Defining poverty
% Agreeing with each definition of poverty

	1983	**1986**	**1989**
Relative to others	67	25	25
Subsistence	26	55	60
Below minimum subsistence		95	95

SOURCE: Derived from *British Social Attitudes Surveys*. *See* note 1. The precise wording of the question changes.

Table 1 illustrates the sharp shift between 1983 and 1986 and reveals how dramatically changes in wording affect such research findings. In 1983, two-thirds accepted the view that 'people in Britain today have enough to eat and wear; the main hardship is not being able to keep up with the living standards most people have'.[3] Only 26 per cent defined poverty as being 'mainly about the shortage of absolute necessities such as food and clothing'. Attitudes appeared to stabilise later in the decade as the question wording was standardised. In 1986 and 1989, only 25 per cent thought poverty could be defined as 'enough to buy the things they really needed, but not enough to buy the things most people take for granted'.[4] The most prevalent definition remains the most austere, insisting on inadequacy of food and basic living needs before the term becomes relevant. The British do like their poor to look the part.

Central to any view of how poverty should be dealt with politically are beliefs about the causes of poverty. If people believe poverty can be prevented – and, as we shall see, this is by no means the universal view – the means for doing so will be derived quite closely from their conception of what drives others into poverty in the first place. Table 2 shows a series of findings from surveys which have used almost identical questions to probe this issue.

TABLE 2
Explanations of poverty (%)

There are people in need because:	1983	1986	1989 (a)	1989 (b)	1990
It's an inevitable part of modern life	25	37	34	24	19
Injustice in our society	32	25	29	30	40
Laziness or lack of willpower	22	19	19	18	19
They have been unlucky	13	11	11	18	10

SOURCE: 1983 figures from J Mack and S Lansley, *Poor Britain*, George Allen and Unwin, 1985. 1986 and 1989(a) figures from *British Social Attitudes Surveys*. See note 1. 1989(b) figures from *Eurobarometer: The Perception of Poverty in Europe*, 1990. See note 20. 1990 figures from H Frayman, *Breadline Britain in the 1990s*, Domino Films/LWT, 1991.

To some extent, the findings in Table 2 would seem to suggest a growing awareness of the structural fault-lines in our society, as injustice rises slowly but distinctly up the league table of explanations. Nonetheless, it is equally clear that both punitive explanations in terms of laziness and inadequacy, and fatalistic acceptance of poverty as the inevitable destiny of a good proportion of their fellow citizens, remain relatively constant through the decade. The problem here is the usual one of such surveys. What do people have in mind when they accede to a diagnosis of injustice? Why do they believe poverty is inevitable? Here we have only the faintest signs of that growing public concern and declining meanness of public spirit that the more optimistic of poverty lobby activists have grasped at in the later Thatcher years.

It is not that people are unconscious of unjustifiable inequalities. A large-scale survey in 1984 found that 70 per cent thought that the distribution of income and wealth in Britain was unfair (over 25 per cent continued to think it fair). But 30 per cent thought nothing could be done about it, even though the report's authors see only a small minority (some 16 per cent) as hard core 'existential fatalists'.[5]

The welfare solution: altruism with strings attached

Let us assume for a moment that many people have come to recognise the presence of substantial poverty in Britain, and that they regard some public intervention to reduce it as necessary and desirable. The crunch comes when they are asked to consider where money ought to be used, either through public spending programmes or from their own pockets. People start with some considerable scepticism about the moral impact of the welfare state. In the hey-day of pre-Thatcherite scroungerphobia, four out of five agreed that too many people depended on welfare, and seven out of ten thought welfare had made people lazy. Even among claimants, a large minority thought 'if there wasn't so much social security people would learn to stand on their own two feet'.[6] During the 1980s, such attitudes appeared to recede. The number who agreed that 'the welfare state makes people less willing nowadays to look after themselves' dropped from 52 per cent in 1983 to 39 per cent in 1989.[7]

But the welfare state is a vast apparatus of expenditure plans. Where do people place their priorities? It has frequently been suggested that the failure of Thatcherism to secure the genuine ideological affections of the British people is nowhere better illustrated than by the recurrent survey findings which show people less and less beguiled by the promise of tax cuts and more and more concerned about the need for refuelled expenditure on public services and welfare. Table 3 shows the response in a series of surveys to a question about this trade-off.

TABLE 3
Choosing between taxes and welfare (%)

	1983	1986	1989
Reduce taxes and spend less on health, education and welfare	9	5	3
Keep taxes and spending on these services at the same level as now	54	44	37
Increase taxes and spend more on health, education, and social benefits	32	46	56

SOURCE: British Social Attitudes: The 7th Report, 1990, p2. *See* note 1.

In the 1960s there was a clear majority for tax cuts. In the 1970s, the notion that 'social services and benefits [had] gone too far and should be cut back a lot' increased steadily, to command the assent of 20 per cent in 1979.[8] Table 3 reveals how, by the 1980s, this pattern had changed significantly. The increase in support for welfare is marked among higher income groups, and recently even registers significantly among Conservative voters.

Of course, general assent to the principle that welfare spending should be increased by means of higher taxes is not the same as a willingness to pay those taxes. In one major survey, one in five of those who supported the general principle were unwilling to fund it themselves.[9] In any case, answers to hypothetical questions from a 'nice lady' with a clipboard are rather different to real demands from the Inland Revenue. Nonetheless, in general the message would seem quite clear. The public has had its fill of the cuts, has resisted the blandishments of the tax-slashers, and wants its welfare state back please. Doesn't it? Well, yes and no. If we look beyond this broad response to the detail of attitudes to spending programmes we encounter a more complex pattern.

Let us assume these expressions of support for welfare spending are just what they seem, and that hypothetical endorsement of a generous tax/welfare trade-off is no less than it seems to be. What kind of expenditure would people support? Table 4 shows the priorities which people select among public expenditure programmes.

TABLE 4
First or second priority for extra government spending (%)

	1983	1985	1989
Health	63	75	84
Education	50	57	55
Industry	29	16	7
Housing	20	21	22
Social security benefits	12	12	14

SOURCE: Compiled from relevant *British Social Attitudes Surveys*. See note 1.

Consistently through the 1980s, only about one in seven people give social security as a first or second priority. Health, education and housing all significantly precede social security in their rankings. In other words, general public services appear more popular than selective or income maintenance provision. Education is notably higher in the rankings of higher income groups, social security in that of lower income groups. But even among the latter (defined as having a household income below £6,000 per year) only 11 per cent gave social security first priority for increased spending in 1989.[10]

This kind of general inquiry, however, is less telling than more detailed questioning about the kind of benefits which people would support. Table 5 shows the support for a range of benefits from a list offered to people in a series of surveys through the 1980s.

TABLE 5
Attitudes to benefits
First or second priority for extra spending from offered list (%)

	1983	1986	1989
Retirement pensions	64	65	67
Child benefit	21	23	30
Benefits for unemployed	33	33	25
Benefits for disabled	57	58	60
Single parents' benefits	21	18	17

SOURCE: Compiled from relevant *British Social Attitudes Surveys*. See note 1.

Benefits for elderly people and people with disabilities consistently receive more support than unemployment benefit and child benefit. Nonetheless, one reading of these results might suggest that the support for benefits for unemployed people is remarkably high, with one-third of respondents giving it first or second priority in 1983 and 1986, though it falls away again at the end of the decade. In fact, by 1989 only 11 per cent chose benefits for unemployed people as their first priority.[11] This support was lowest among manual workers, always the least generous in their views of those on benefits outside the labour market, and distinctly lower among Conservative voters.[12]

Support for child benefit is, predictably, differentiated by age. In 1989, 69 per cent of the 25-34 age group gave child benefit first or second priority, while only 20 per cent of the over-55s did so. Attitudes to child benefit are undoubtedly influenced by more general views on family life and the role of women. In 1987, 48 per cent agreed that 'a husband's job is to earn the money; a wife's job is to look after the family and home'.[13] An increasing proportion (29 per cent), however, agree that a married woman with children under school age should work outside the home 'if she needs the money'. Self-interest and moral judgement jostle uncomfortably in the public psyche when pressed for opinions concerning public expenditure or about women's roles.

Such moral judgments are, of course, central in any public assessment of the utility or appropriateness of benefits. While the wilder excesses of scroungerphobia charted in the late 1970s and early 1980s have been muted by the sombre realities of Thatcherite reconstruction, they have never really disappeared. The number of people who agreed that 'the welfare state makes people less willing to look after themselves' fell from 52 per cent in 1983 to 39 per cent in 1989; but in 1989, 28 per cent still believed that 'many people who get social security don't deserve any help'. Between 1983 and 1986 the number who agreed strongly that 'large numbers of people falsely claim benefits' actually rose from 40 per cent to 45 per cent – almost as many as the number who suggested that 'large numbers of people who are eligible for benefits fail to claim them' (49 per cent in 1986).[14] Indeed, as many as 65 per cent agreed either strongly or slightly with the first of these views. Again, this scepticism about claimant honesty is highest among Conservative voters and manual workers. Curiously, concern about both issues seems to have increased through the decade, suggesting a general discontent with the effectiveness of the benefit system coupled with a resilient doubt about the probity of claimants. These attitudes are summarised in Table 6.

TABLE 6
Attitudes to social security claimants (%)

	Agree	Disagree
Many people who get social security don't really deserve any help	28	45
Most people on the dole are fiddling one way or another	31	37
Around here, most people could find a job if they really wanted one	52	28

SOURCE: *British Social Attitudes: The 7th Report,* 1990, p11. *See* note 1.

Doubts about the real needs of claimants are highest among Conservative voters and elderly people. More interestingly, the number who believe claimants are on the fiddle rises significantly as we move down the social scale. While 24 per cent of professional workers think most people on the dole are fiddling, this rises to 38 per cent among unskilled manual workers.[15] The divisiveness of the moral order created by inadequate benefits and punitively low incomes in work remains a potent source of disdain and distrust among working poor people about those who reside threateningly just beneath them on the economic ladder.

Euromyths: British attitudes compared

The way we perceive, explain, and address poverty is deeply rooted in the particular social history, Poor Law tradition and current fortunes of our own nation. The UK's social security system took its first inspiration from Bismarckian origins and, as the moves towards harmonisation across the European Community have become steadily more overt in recent years, it has been salutary to examine how attitudes to social security and poverty in this country compare with those at the other end of the Channel Tunnel.

It is usually assumed that the UK remains firmly embedded in the European social democratic tradition of welfare statism. Indeed, this is the general conclusion of major comparative attitude studies.[16] This remained true even as the government turned ever more insistently to the horizon across the Atlantic for inspiration on social policy (see Chapter 2). In the middle of the decade, a composite question designed to elicit the degree of support for a redistributive welfare strategy[17] found around 60 to 70 per cent of people in favour of redistribution in European countries, including 63 per cent in Britain, while in the USA the figure was distinctly lower, at 38 per cent.[18] At first blush, then, little to distinguish us from those 'civilised chaps' on the Continent who seem, as we patronisingly assured ourselves, belatedly to be acquiring our hallowed traditions of clean drinking water and looking after the less fortunate.

Closer inspection suggests that, in fact – much like the shock which came with the discovery that it was our drinking water, not theirs, which needed the health warning – so too our attitudes to poverty looked a little murky when set alongside those of other Europeans. Two major studies by the European Commission in 1976 and 1989 examined the perception of poverty in Europe. Though limited methodologically,[19] they do offer some guide to comparative attitudes. Poverty is far less visible in the UK than in other countries. Fewer people in the UK than any other nationality, with the exception of Luxembourg, believe that people in their locality are poor.[20] Yet, as Chapter 5 observes, the increase in the number of poor people in the European Community in the period 1980-85 was in fact contributed to overwhelmingly by the UK.

Table 7 shows the explanations offered by people in each country for the existence of poverty, using the four choices common in many such surveys. Over time, there has been a very significant movement in these figures. Denmark is the only country in which more people in 1989 offered laziness as an explanation for why people are poor than did so in 1976. The UK was outstandingly the most ungenerous and punitive in its attitudes in 1976, when 43 per cent suggested laziness as the main reason and only 16 per cent suggested social injustice. As Table 7 shows, by the late 1980s this had been reversed and people in the UK had moved into line, at least on this issue and on this way of measuring it.

This reversal seems to be related partly to the rapid growth in poverty and inequality in the UK. Despite their apparent imperviousness to poverty in their area, more people in the UK than in any other country believe the gap between rich and poor is growing.[21]

TABLE 7
Comparing two explanations of poverty offered in different European countries (%)

	Laziness/lack of willpower	Social injustice
Belgium	14	22
Denmark	18	15
Germany	19	34
France	14	29
Ireland	14	30
Italy	23	41
Luxembourg	25	25
Netherlands	10	20
United Kingdom	18	30
EEC	17	32

SOURCE: *Eurobarometer: The Perception of Poverty in Europe*, 1990, p37. *See* note 20.

These findings should be treated with great care. The apparent turn-round in UK attitudes to a more social and altruistic vision has frequently been gratefully extracted from this research by anxious campaigners eager to find fertile soil on which to sow. Another table from the same research, however, immediately casts doubt on this conclusion. Table 8 shows the answers to a question in the 1989 EC survey about the most common reasons for people being poor.

In these figures, people in the UK still seem to consider laziness more likely an explanation than those in other countries. Indeed, the very poverty and limited educational opportunities which character-ise the UK seem to be strongly associated with this distribution of attitudes. It is, in other words, poverty, inequality, and limited oppor-tunities which breed mistrust and moral parsimony, rather than any mystical trait in the national character. For example, when asked about additional public spending on unemployment benefits, the divide between low- and high-income groups was sharper in the UK than in other countries surveyed. While 59 per cent in the UK in the poorest quartile favoured an increase, only 25 per cent among the wealthiest quartile were as keen. In Italy, the gap was 63:52; in Germany, 41:19.[22]

TABLE 8
'Why are people poor?' (%)

	Belg	Den	Ger	Fra	Ire	Ita	Neth	UK	EEC
Long-term unemployment	51	52	43	66	64	52	55	60	53
Alcoholism/drugs	35	44	58	31	39	37	50	22	38
Sickness	30	51	42	32	25	32	24	18	30
Broken families	30	43	28	17	33	29	41	38	27
Deprived upbringing	28	6	20	21	25	26	16	23	23
Welfare cuts	19	20	19	17	40	13	42	33	20
Laziness	18	15	18	16	16	19	11	21	17

SOURCE: Compiled from *Eurobarometer: The Perception of Poverty in Europe*, 1990, pp40-41. *See* note 20.

As we have seen, attitudes to poverty are shaped in part by what it is that people regard as an acceptable or minimum standard of living. Figures on this are almost impossible to compare. But it does appear that people in the UK have lower expectations about what should be considered a necessity than most other nations. For example, having a car or an annual holiday is considered a necessity by most people in Europe but by only a minority in the UK. Indeed, the *Breadline Britain* surveys suggest fewer people thought a holiday an essential in 1990 than in 1983 (54 per cent compared to 63 per cent). Using material from these and other surveys, Table 9 shows how people responded to these two questions, perhaps suggesting just how little can be deduced from such research.

TABLE 9
'Are these necessities?' (%)

	BB 1983	BB 1990	EEC 1989	
			UK	EEC
Car	22	26	20	35
Annual holiday	63	54	31	43

SOURCE: Derived from *Poor Britain*, 1985; *Breadline Britain in the 1990s*, 1991; relevant *British Social Attitudes Surveys*; and *Eurobarometer: Perceptions of Poverty in Europe*, 1990. *See* notes 1 and 20, and source notes to Table 2.

Perhaps saddest of all is the finding that the UK offers the highest proportion of people with pessimistic views about chances of escaping from poverty.[23] The British are sceptical about their poor, austere in what they think constitutes an essential standard of living and less than optimistic that things will change.

Images of poverty: victims and vandals

In the decade of *Boys from the Blackstuff* and *Eastenders*, it is hard to suggest that attitudes to poverty are fed remorselessly by images of the kind that created the anti-scrounger hysteria of the late 1970s. In the face of fast-rising unemployment in the recession of the early 1980s, and the growing polarisation that followed it, more complex and contradictory images began to surface in the media and in public debate. It is not possible here to review that process, but for the purposes of this book there are two salient issues.

First, the role of charity has rapidly changed in the decade, and with it the kind of images and rhetoric about poverty injected into public consciousness. With the growing sense of a need to soften the harsher corners of Thatcherism, the vision of the 'active citizen' has been sedulously cultivated, fired by an altruistic urge fuelled by gratitude for the largesse derived from the benefits of free market enterprise. The role of charities has grown enormously, notably, of course, since the social fund began to bite. In turn, charities have grown in number, and have become increasingly professional and business-like in style and performance. At the same time, business leaders seeking spiritual reward in the hereafter – or knighthoods in the here and now – have signed up with the PerCent Club and, in the words of its first chairman, Sir Hector Laing of United Biscuits, have 'taken over the modern guise of the city fathers'.

The media have provided a highly successful vehicle for the new model charities. Telethon, Children in Need and Comic Relief are the market leaders. This is big business. With a total annual income of £16 billion, the voluntary sector takes a sizeable 4 per cent of GNP. Expenditure on advertising by charities has trebled in the last six years and, since 1989, has been eligible for airtime on television, ending a 34-year ban.

The paradox for the government is that in unleashing the charitable tiger it has barely held on to its tail. The land is alight with stark and forceful images of homelessness, child abuse, the old, the sick and the lonely as the iconographers of plenty have been let loose on the underside of Thatcherite Britain. A crucial feature of this hard-nosed new order in the charity world is a much sharper and more aggressive political style. The 1990 Telethon, for example, included 80-second films by agency Bartle Bogle Hegarty, featuring rent boys and homeless families comparing their lives with life in a prison cell.

The final irony is that, for all this effort, people are giving less to charity. The latest *Charity Trends* notes that 'the *typical* donor over the last twelve months only gave £1.28 per month whereas in the previous twelve months he or she gave £1.97'.[24] Despite the millions garnered by the late night TV extravaganzas (£22 million for Children in Need, £24 million for Telethon), public generosity in the aggregate has been as yet little troubled by the new charity image-making. Indeed another worry surfaces. As Diana Leat notes, 'Rolling scoreboards emblazoned in lights, cheers at every further thousand pounds, do little to foster public awareness that the amount of money raised is merely a means to and not the end of the exercise.'[25] It may, however, reflect growing public awareness of the public squalor amid private affluence which is the stock-in-trade of the charitable appeal. The surveys conducted for the Charities Aid Foundation suggest that a large majority (83 per cent in 1990) think that the government ought to help more and not rely on charities to provide the money for those in need.[26]

The second feature of 1980s imagery is of the celebration of the new consumerism, from designer socialism in the glossy pages of *Marxism Today* to the exotic travel ads of the Sunday colour supplements. That we have never had it so good may have been the rallying cry of Macmillan's supervision of post-war affluence, but it became a desperate assertion against the evidence in the increasingly divided times of the Thatcher decade, all the more insistently trumpeted for all that. The 1986 edition of *Social Trends* found itself the front page lead in the *Daily Express* under the headline, 'It's better and better to be British.'[27] This story, not untypical of the celebratory tone of so much social reportage in the 1980s, informed readers that 'The Great British public has never had it so good. People now have more money in their pockets than ever before. And that is official.'

Yet, at the same time, exposure and explanation of poverty became increasingly marginalised. The London Weekend Television documentary series, *Breadline Britain,* in its second incarnation in

1991, found its first showing televised at the dead of night, and it became increasingly difficult to excite interest and concern about what now seemed tired images and yesterday's troubles. Meanwhile, the treatment of claimants, and especially social security abuse, has continued to sustain a climate of suspicion and scorn which, if it lacked the venom and scale of a few years earlier, has lost nothing in potent mythology. Headlines such as 'Hit Squad to trap Scroungers' (*Daily Mail*),[28] 'Scroungers will be Nicked – It's War on the Loadsa-money Lot' (*Daily Star*)[29] or 'War on the Something for Nothing Brigade – Big Welfare Crackdown' (*Sun*),[30] still regularly decorate the tabloids. Meanwhile, their coverage of other aspects of social security – notably their virtual silence on the Fowler reviews and subsequent legislation – is conspicuous in its absence.

Conclusion

Attitudes to poverty are contradictory and complex and no summary such as this, largely based on national social surveys, can adequately review the full range and intricacy of this aspect of public opinion. However, some messages for future work in changing attitudes may just dimly be glimpsed amid this somewhat untidy evidence:

- First, people's attitudes are intimately bound up with their own circumstances and fortunes. The fate of those ill-rewarded in the labour market will continue to set a ceiling for raising public sympathy for more generous benefits. Campaigning on low-pay issues in tandem with benefit issues will therefore be essential.
- Second, poverty is still, and perhaps increasingly, invisible. The simple facts of living standards, benefit rates, and social exclusion among the poorest section of the community are little known and need to be better understood.
- Third, we cannot afford to be complacent because of too optimistic a reading of research which seems to suggest that the message of Thatcherism has fallen on deaf ears. While it is true that vestiges of support for welfare are still operative, they are highly conditional and focused, and easily dislodged.
- Fourth, poverty is not a thing apart, nor is its continuation inevitable. Images of the possible as well as of the desirable need to be fostered to recognise that what has been done so success-

fully for the wealthy in the last ten years could equally be done for the poor.

• Finally, the lesson is clearly that a genuine approach to citizenship for all has to be expressed in terms which, as Ruth Lister has argued, allow it to act 'as an inspiration once more to those who believe in a society built on the foundations of justice and democratic participation'.[31] To recapture this high ground is the task for those concerned about the patterns of public attitudes and determined to make them poor no more.

Notes

1. Inevitably this chapter draws heavily on the findings of the British Social Attitudes surveys, conducted annually by Social and Community Planning Research since 1983. All are published in London by Gower. The full references are: R Jowell and C Airey (eds), *British Social Attitudes: The 1984 Report,* 1984; R Jowell and S Witherspoon (eds), *British Social Attitudes: the 1985 report,* 1985; R Jowell, S Witherspoon and L Brook (eds), *British Social Attitudes: The 1986 Report,* 1986; R Jowell, S Witherspoon and L Brook (eds), *British Social Attitudes: The 1987 Report,* 1987; R Jowell, S Witherspoon and L Brook (eds), *British Social Attitudes: The 5th Report,* 1988; R Jowell, S Witherspoon and L Brook (eds), *British Social Attitudes: The 6th Report – Special International Edition,* 1989; R Jowell, S Witherspoon and L Brook, *British Social Attitudes: The 7th Report,* 1990.
2. *British Social Attitudes: The 1987 Report,* p9. *See* note 1.
3. *British Social Attitudes: The 7th Report,* p8. *See* note 1.
4. *See* note 3.
5. G Marshal *et al, Social Class in Modern Britain,* Hutchinson, 1988, p158.
6. P Golding and S Middleton, *Images of Welfare: Press and Public Attitudes to Poverty,* Martin Robertson, 1982, p167.
7. *British Social Attitudes: The 1984 Report; British Social Attitudes: The 7th Report. See* note 1.
8. P Taylor-Gooby, *Public Opinion, Ideology and State Welfare,* Routledge and Kegan Paul, 1985, pp25-27.
9. *See* note 5, p174.
10. *See* note 3, p8.
11. *See* note 3, p4.
12. *See* note 3, p23.
13. *British Social Attitudes: The 5th Report,* p189. *See* note 1.
14. *See* note 2, p8.
15. *See* note 3, p26.
16. *British Social Attitudes: The 6th Report – Special International Edition,* p65. *See* note 1.
17. Comprised of five items: 'reduce differences in income', provide a job for everyone who wants one, spend less on benefits for the poor (disagree), provide

a decent standard of living for unemployed people, and provide everyone with a guaranteed basic income.

18. *See* note 16, p62.
19. *See* P Golding, 'In the eye of the beholder', in *Europe Against Poverty Volume II: Cross-National Studies,* Espoir, 1980.
20. Commission of the European Communities, *Eurobarometer: The Perception of Poverty in Europe,* Brussels, Paper V/467/90-EN, 1990, p25.
21. *See* note 20, p96.
22. *See* note 16, p50.
23. *See* note 20.
24. M Brophy, 'Foreword', in *Charity Trends: 13th Edition,* Charities Aid Foundation, 1990, p4.
25. D Leat, 'Broadcast appeals: quantitative measures of success', in *Charity Trends: 13th Edition,* p148. *See* note 24.
26. *See* note 24, p34.
27. *Daily Express,* 9 January 1986.
28. *Daily Mail,* 16 May 1986.
29. *Daily Star,* 12 May 1988.
30. *Sun,* 21 September 1987.
31. R Lister, *Citizens All?,* Inaugural Lecture, University of Bradford, 1990, pp44-45.

5.
A time for change

Graham Room

THIS chapter examines some of the major economic, demographic and social changes that are likely to take place during the 1990s, as they relate to people living on low incomes. The focus is upon the United Kingdom, but seen in relation to the other countries of Western Europe with which this country is becoming increasingly integrated. The chapter then takes stock of some of the principal policy options that could re-shape the map of poverty, in particular at the European Community (EC) level.

Poverty and change in the 1980s

During the 1980s, the EC sponsored a growing number of studies of people living on relatively low incomes. These studies were undertaken principally within the framework of the EC anti-poverty programmes of 1975-80, 1986-89 and 1990-94 which, although consisting mainly of action projects, also involved some statistical and research work. These revealed three principal developments against which the situation in the United Kingdom can be set.[1]

The numbers of people living on relatively low incomes

In 1987, within the framework of the EC's second anti-poverty programme, O'Higgins and Jenkins used a poverty line set at 50 per cent of average equivalent disposable income in each of the twelve member states taken separately. They estimated the numbers of people in the EC who were living on relatively low incomes in the mid-1980s to be 44 million, an increase of 4.5 million since the beginning of the decade.[2] More recently, using data based on household expenditure not income, Teekens has produced an even higher estimate for 1985 – 50 million people.[3] But his estimates reveal stability in this global figure during the first half of the decade.

These figures suggest that more than one in eight of the citizens of the EC are now living in severely restricted financial circumstances, as judged by the standard of living in their own country. However, the same figures provide conflicting evidence as to whether, for the Community as a whole, the proportion of people on low incomes was increasing during the 1980s, a decade in which unemployment was high internationally.

Both sets of figures have been politically controversial, particularly as inter-country comparisons of poverty rates. However, they are in broad agreement that, as judged against the EC as a whole, the UK's position in the poverty league table deteriorated during the first half of the decade. Teekens demonstrates that the increase in the number of poor persons in the Community in the period 1980-85 is contributed to overwhelmingly by the UK; the O'Higgins and Jenkins estimates also highlight the UK as a country in which the poverty rate worsened dramatically in this period.[4]

The numbers of people receiving means-tested assistance

During much of the 1980s, in the UK and elsewhere, the size of the population dependent in whole or in part upon state financial support was substantially higher than in the 1970s. Typical increases in the numbers of beneficiaries or recipients of national means-tested assistance (for example, income support in this country) were 400 per cent in Belgium (1976-89); 140 per cent in the Federal Republic of Germany (1978-89); 42 per cent in the Republic of Ireland (1976-89); and 37 per cent in the Netherlands (1975-89). Rates of take-up of these means-tested benefits in other EC countries have commonly been worse than in the UK; and these figures therefore underestimate the numbers of people eligible.[5] But the figures do not enable us to distinguish between increasing numbers of people in difficulty and the changes in the numbers of people who are eligible for benefit as the conditions of entitlement change.

The changing composition of the low-income population

Across the Community as a whole, the 1980s saw several major changes in the composition of the low-income population.

The first change that took place in the 1980s was that unemployed people came to form a much larger proportion of the poor and of those on social assistance than they did in the 1970s. But it is not only through unemployment that changes in the labour market have re-shaped the map of poverty. The numbers of those who are employed but who are poor or who depend on social assistance also increased in several countries.[6] (See Chapter 3 for a full discussion of the effects of employment and unemployment changes on the map of poverty in the UK.)

Second, although in many countries elderly people are still at high risk of being on low incomes, this risk is considerably less than was the case 10 or 15 years ago, largely because of improvements in pension schemes. Elderly people form a declining proportion of the low-income population, something that is the more remarkable given that, in the EC countries generally, they make up an increasing proportion of the population as a whole. In Germany, for example, the proportion of households dependent upon social assistance who were elderly fell from 40 per cent in 1970 to only 13 per cent in 1986. Less dramatic falls can also be traced for the UK.

Nevertheless, elderly people remain in many countries the largest single 'category' of people who are poor or receiving social assistance. Moreover, despite the general improvement in their living standards, there are substantial disparities of income and welfare between the 'young old' and the 'very old'. A much larger proportion of the very old are women, who have traditionally gained lower pensions and benefits than men. Equally serious is the prospect for today's long-term unemployed people when they eventually retire. Their interrupted work and contribution records are likely to mean that the unemployment which separated them from the bulk of the working population during their working lives will, during the 1990s and beyond, turn them into the 'new poor' of the elderly population.

The third set of changes in the population of poor people has been connected with changes in family structure. The major change, evident in all the countries of the Community, is the growth in the number of lone-parent families, who are at serious risk of poverty. In many countries, their employment opportunities have declined as a result of cuts in childcare facilities. At the same time, attempts in countries like France to provide alternative social protection for lone parents have been surrounded by controversy. This is mostly because of fears that such protection will create disincentives to work or to marriage. The result, according to Eurostat (the statistical office of the EC) is that in the 1980s all EC countries except the Netherlands had poverty rates for female-headed households higher than for the population as a whole.[7] However, in the UK at least, the extent to which the risk of poverty for lone-parent families exceeds that for the general population depends heavily upon the poverty line which is used, with many living on the margins of poverty.[8]

Again, according to Eurostat, 'in the majority of the EC member states children became relatively worse off during the period 1980-85', and in four member states there was an actual increase in the numbers of poor children: the Netherlands, Ireland, Germany and the UK.[9]

Change in the 1990s

These developments suggest that four main factors were re-shaping the map of poverty during the 1980s:

- *Demographic changes* – most obviously, the increasing numbers of elderly people.
- *Social changes* – notably the rising rates of family dissolution.
- *Economic changes* – helping to shape the rate and pattern of employment and unemployment.
- *Changes in social benefits* – notably the increasing use of means-tested benefits.[10]

How are these factors likely to develop during the 1990s, in the UK and in the EC as a whole? And what new factors may become important?

The ageing population

People are living longer, but fewer children are being born. The likely effects of these two developments are well known. Fewer young people are coming on to the labour market – for the EC as a whole, between now and 2025, the expectation is of a drop from 23 per cent to 18 per cent in the proportion of the population aged 15-24. During the same period, the proportion of the population aged over 64 is expected to rise from 14.4 per cent to 19.3 per cent.

These changes are more extreme than those expected in the United States and Japan, our main trading rivals, and still more than countries of south-east Asia. They suggest that the EC will face more acutely the challenge of supporting an expanding elderly population and a reduced inflow of young recruits to the needs of a dynamic and changing economy.[11] Nevertheless, these effects should not be over-stated, at least not for the UK. Here, during the period until 2010, the proportion of the total population which is of working age (20-59) is expected to fall only slightly, from 53.4 per cent to 52.1 per cent.[12]

The costs and benefits of these developments are difficult to predict, as are their likely consequences for patterns of disadvantage. The consequences include increasing demands being placed on infor-mal carers, the majority of whom are women. They also include the social expenditure costs on working-age people of a dependent population: a strain which might be reduced by shifting the cost on to that population itself, through lower levels of pension. But the extent of these costs will depend significantly upon developments in the typical age of retirement and in the age of onset of frailty, as well as upon the extent of increases in female employment, boosting the size of the working population.[13]

The increasing numbers of lone parents

It is still more difficult to predict trends in the numbers of lone-parent families during the 1990s and beyond. They now account for around 10 per cent of all families with children in France, Belgium, Germany and the Netherlands, and close to 15 per cent in the UK. Moreover, a sharper rise is projected over the next quarter of a century: the UK government, for example, has estimated that by the year 2005 there will be 2.8 million lone-parent families, compared with just over 1 million in the mid-1980s.[14]

Labour market participation by lone parents varies greatly between countries. In Germany and France, their rates of labour market participation are as high as 60 per cent and 75 per cent respectively, well above the UK figure. But in such countries as Denmark, higher rates of unemployment for lone parents during the 1980s arose in part from cuts in childcare facilities and policies leading to disproportionately high female unemployment.

Poverty studies in the EC countries show that lone-parent families experience substantially more poverty than other family types. There seems every reason to expect that they will continue to rely significantly on state financial support. What is more open to question is the extent to which tighter requirements will be placed upon lone parents to be 'actively seeking work' or pursuing training as a condition of such financial support, as is commonly the case among our EC partners.

Rates and patterns of unemployment

The European Commission, in a recent study of employment trends and prospects, highlights four main trends across the EC as a whole during recent years:
- A surge in the late 1980s in the numbers of jobs created (especially in the UK, Denmark and the Iberian countries).
- The increase in female employment.
- The high proportion of part-time jobs within this expansion.
- The concentration of these part-time jobs within the service sector.

It is in the Federal Republic, the industrial power-house of the Community, that this shift to the service sector has been slowest, while the UK (and Luxembourg) have suffered the greatest decline in employment in manufacturing.

In general, the new jobs created have been filled by young people coming on to the labour market, and by an increase in female participation rates (notably in the Federal Republic), rather than by unemployed people generally – but with the UK and Portugal as partial exceptions to this rule. For the Community as a whole, the conclusion which the European Commission draws is that, even with slower increases in the working-age population during the 1990s, 'a massive and continuing expansion in employment will almost certainly be necessary in order to reduce unemployment to more acceptable levels over the coming years'.[15]

Is this likely to happen? The Commission is optimistic about the overall stimulus to economic and employment growth which is likely to be provided by the Single Market – but particular regions and countries may suffer.[16] The prospects for UK industry in particular are not good.[17] Here, only around one-third of manufacturing employment is in sectors having a strong trading performance and competitive edge – on a par with Spain and Greece, but much lower than in the more prosperous EC countries. It is unlikely that the structural funds of the Commission – designed in part to assist areas threatened by unemployment – will be of a sufficient scale to compensate for these negative effects of the Single Market.

In its forecasts for the UK over the next two decades, the Policy Studies Institute expects that, with the continuing growth in service sector employment, and taking into account the demographic developments mentioned earlier, unemployment in the UK will fall steadily through the second half of the 1990s.[18] Nevertheless, these expectations could be undermined if the threat to manufacturing employment is as serious as Commission studies appear to suggest.

It must be hazardous to predict the net outcome of these various developments for rates of poverty. The Statistical Office of the European Commission has recently been sponsoring research into methodologies for predicting poverty rates on the basis of broad social and economic variables, but these efforts are still incomplete. In any case, during the 1990s, various new factors are liable to become important in shaping the map of disadvantage in the EC countries.

Principal among these are likely to be higher rates of migration that develop between the EC countries and, at least as important, from eastern Europe. These population shifts could significantly alter the patterns of employment and unemployment in the EC countries and of dependence upon their social security systems. Liberalisation of laws on emigration from the Soviet Union could dramatically increase such effects.[19] Germany is most likely to be affected. However, in the other countries of the EC these migration inflows have so far been much more modest and it remains to be seen how widely their effects will be spread. As far as the UK is concerned, the other source of potential immigration could be Hong Kong.[20]

Social policy options and their 'Europeanisation'

It seems likely that, increasingly, many of the principal factors shaping the map of poverty will move outside the control of individual national governments. This is most obviously the case in relation to economic and employment growth, with the 'globalisation' of economic functioning.[21] But will social policy responses also become a matter for supra-national and inter-governmental coordination, or will they remain jealously guarded as a national preserve?

More specifically, what are the prospects that social policies will be 'Europeanised'? What will determine the areas of social policy which are most likely to become a Community concern, with the regulation, funding or administration of policies and programmes being transferred from national authorities to the EC institutions? And how far will poverty and disadvantage come to figure within EC policy concerns?

Leibfried, in an examination of anti-poverty policies, has argued that policies directed at those groups of the population which enjoy the highest degree of moral credibility will most readily be 'Europeanised'.[22] In particular, he gives the example of the 'elderly poor' as enjoying greater moral credibility than, for example, the 'unemployed poor', who are often stigmatised as 'work-shy'. He argues that it will, therefore, be the 'disreputable poor' who are left behind at a national level; and that the national policies which are left to deal with them are likely to receive lower priority within the national social budget. He warns, finally, that the result may be to create an 'underclass' which is ghettoised within each country and excluded from any real participation in the new emerging forms of European citizenship (an issue returned to in Chapter 7).

Leibfried is posing some important questions and his analysis of the consequences of shifting levels of policy-making for different population groups is illuminating. Nevertheless, in forecasting which population groups and programmes are most likely to be deemed suitable for attention at Community level, it is necessary to take into account the specific legal and political framework within which EC policy-making is being developed. Under the Treaty of Rome and the Single European Act, the legal base for the institutions of the Community to act in the social policy field is, of course, very restricted. In the face of these restrictions, Community decision-makers have resurrected the ecclesiastical doctrine of 'subsidiarity', under which Community action in the social field must in general be subordinate to that of the national authorities, save where specific measures are required to support the functioning of the Single Market and to compensate for the social dislocations which it could produce.[23]

Policies for unemployed people, for example, would then seem more likely to be raised to Community level, not because of their moral credibility or lack of it, but rather because employment is already, to some extent at least, within the recognised field of concern of the Community institutions. In addition, it is clear that action on unemployment could fairly readily be justified in relation to the Single Market and its socio-economic consequences. In this case, it would be elderly people and other groups unrelated to the labour market who would be 'left behind', to be supported at a national level. However, if they continue to enjoy the high moral credibility which Leibfried indicates, they will presumably be less likely to suffer the progressive deterioration in treatment which he foresees for those who remain a purely national concern.

The European Community's Charter of Fundamental Social Rights of Workers (more commonly known as the Social Charter), is concerned, as its name suggests, primarily with workers.[24] But how far are social rights divisible, in the sense that the rights of those at work and the rights of those outside can be dealt with in isolation from each other? This raises the larger question of citizenship rights at a Community level and the extent to which these will, as in the Bismarckian tradition, be tied to work status and record. At a further level, as Chapter 7 shows, the Charter excludes 'non-citizens', many of whom will be people from ethnic minorities. The development of all these rights will depend upon the new constellations of political interests that emerge at national and Community level under the impulse of the Single Market, and cannot with any confidence be forecast at this stage.[25]

Notes

1. Commission of the European Communities, *Final Report on the Second European Poverty Programme*, Com (91) 29, 1991.

2. M O'Higgins and S Jenkins, *Poverty in Europe: Estimates for the Numbers in Poverty in 1975, 1980, 1985,* paper presented at EC Seminar on Poverty Statistics, 1989.

3. Commission of the European Communities, *Inequality and Poverty in Europe (1980-1985),* (Eurostat Rapid Reports), Statistical Office, 1990.

4. Compare with J Northcott, *Britain in 2010,* Policy Studies Institute, 1991, pp283-4.

5. G Room *et al, National Policies to Combat Social Exclusion,* Commission of the European Communities, 1991.

6. Compare with G Room *et al,'New Poverty' in the European Community,* Macmillan, 1990, Chapter 6.

7.   *See* note 3.
8.   *See* note 6, Chapter 5.
9.   *See* note 3.
10. *See* note 4, pp284-5.
11. Commission of the European Communities, *Employment in Europe*, 1990, Chapter 1.
12. *See* note 4, p133.
13. P Johnson, *The Costs and Benefits of Population Ageing,* paper presented to the International Colloquium on Opportunities and Challenges in an Ageing Society, Amsterdam, 26-28 October 1989; compare with C Gillion, 'Ageing populations: spreading the costs', *Journal of European Social Policy,* Vol 1, No 2, November 1991.
14. Family Policy Studies Centre, *Fact Sheet 3: One Parent Families,* 1986, p2.
15. *See* note 11, p25.
16. *See* note 11, Chapter 3.
17. *See* note 4, Chapter 16.
18. *See* note 4, Chapter 13.
19. V Ronge, 'Social change in eastern Europe', in *Journal of European Social Policy*, Vol 1, No 1, August 1991.
20. *See* note 4, p130.
21. *See* note 4, Chapter 4 and Foreword.
22. S Leibfried, *European Welfare Regimes in Transition,* paper presented to the EC Seminar on Poverty, Marginalisation and Social Exclusion, Alghero, April 1990.
23. P Spicker, 'The principle of subsidiarity and the social policy of the European Community', in *Journal of European Social Policy,* Vol 1, No 1, August 1991.
24. *See* note 11.
25. P Lange, *The Politics of the Social Dimension: interests, states and redistribution in the 1992 process* (unpublished), Duke University, 1990.

6.

Towards welfare rights

Pete Alcock

THIS chapter discusses the development of welfare rights work over the last two decades and the challenges it has faced from the policy changes of the 1980s. It argues that rights to welfare, across the range of public, private and voluntary services, are likely to be a central issue in policy development in the 1990s. This chapter advocates a rights-based strategy for welfare by the next government.

Rights and discretion

Much of the state welfare which we continue to experience in Britain today was established during the period of social reform which followed the Second World War. Despite the changes which have since been imposed, with increasing rapidity, upon the post-war welfare state, its basic structure has remained the framework within which welfare services have largely been delivered and received. However, the idea of a 'right' to welfare was a notion which, despite the ideals of Beveridge[1] and Marshall[2] who each promoted their respective philosophies in this area, only achieved partial recognition within the structures of post-war state welfare.

Rights were recognised as important within the national insurance system, state education and the National Health Service (NHS). Indeed, following the establishment of the NHS people were actively encouraged to take up their rights to free treatment, since many were slow to believe in their right to state provision without direct payment. But elsewhere in the post-war welfare state, rights to services often gave way to discretionary provision based upon the judgements of state bureaucrats and professionals.

In care services, such as social work, this professionalism – and particularly 'professional judgements' – operated to *exclude* clients from rights to services. Similarly, local authority housing, though reputedly intended to be available to all, was in practice allocated not by right but at the discretion of local authorities and their housing officers. In cash services, such as social security, the growth of the vast, imposing and impersonal Department of Social Security (DSS), with its complicated forms, intimidating offices and bureaucracy, has contributed to what is often a poor quality service, and the alienation of claimants.[3] The ever-increasing reliance upon means-tested benefits as a method of 'targeting' money to those in greatest need and as a means for controlling expenditure has led to high levels of non-take-up of benefits, effectively excluding many people who *do* have acknowledged rights to payments. Indeed, means-testing is experienced by many claimants as a system of exclusion from rights – a way of 'keeping people out', rather than a method of letting them in.

The distinction between rights on the one hand and discretion and/or means-testing on the other, as a gateway to rights of social security, was centrally inscribed in the major institutions of state welfare. In the forty years following the evolution of the welfare state, the discretion and paternalism associated with bureaucracy and professionalism have come to play an increasingly dominant role within many welfare services. This contributed to the alienating impact of welfare provision, which by the 1970s was becoming the focus of criticism from both the Left and the Right.

The growth of welfare rights

Ironically, perhaps, the exclusion caused by means-tested social security – and in particular its failure to deliver benefits to those entitled to them – alongside reactions against the paternalism of professional social work, provided part of the basis for the growth of welfare rights work.

Welfare rights work became increasingly important during the 1970s and 1980s, as dependence on means-tested benefits mushroomed.[4] The roots of this expansion lay partly within the social work profession. In particular there was a reaction against the paternalism inherent in the casework approach to social services which often focused on individual and family behaviour or attitudes, rather than on social systems and entitlements.[5]

Other roots lay in the community development and local anti-poverty projects of the 1970s and 1980s.[6] These aimed to challenge local poverty and deprivation by focusing on the failings of existing state welfare services, and worked with local people in order to ameliorate or overcome such deprivation. Projects were largely based outside existing state welfare institutions, although they derived funding and support from them.[7] Many of those involved found they could do relatively little to overcome the poverty faced by local people. But, through advice and advocacy work – the promotion of welfare rights and in particular the take-up of benefits – they could challenge some of the failings of welfare institutions. From the outset, CPAG played an important role, both in providing the tools for such work, via the production of guides to benefits, and in leading the legal challenge to the administration of social security, through the legal test case strategy.[8] In addition, local CPAG branches often provided a geographical focus for welfare rights work and campaigning.

At its most successful, welfare rights work was able to win significant additional resources for poor people[9] and force governments to respond to the legal demands of welfare claimants.[10] Welfare rights workers were also able to challenge some of the previous practices of welfare professionals, since the advocacy approach adopted by welfare rights could act to empower clients in their dealings with welfare institutions. It was argued by some that this 'rights-based' strategy should serve as an example for users of all welfare services, not only the DSS.[11] However, there were others who suggested that welfare rights could merely add to professional power, creating welfare rights professionals who took charge of activities, working *for* poor people rather than *with* them. This could be regarded as reinforcing dependency.[12]

Welfare rights under attack

By the mid-1980s, welfare rights was a growing force within, and without, state welfare. Three-fifths of local authority welfare rights teams operating in 1986, for example, had been created in the previous four years.[13] However, the ethos behind the welfare rights movement was in stark contrast to the 'retreat from state welfare' policies of the Thatcher governments. As Chapter 2 shows, government responses to the failings of state welfare emphasised the provision of rights and choices but via a contractual model, whereby *some* individuals would be empowered to purchase services in a growing market of private welfare.

Welfare rights provided a challenge to this strategy, as well as to the failings of state welfare itself. Successful advocacy of the needs and rights of service users created pressure for more, and improved, services – not cuts. This was particularly the case with the supplementary benefits scheme which had been restructured on a basis of legal entitlements in 1980, following advice offered to the Labour government in the 1970s.[14] However, as rights were increasingly taken up during the 1980s, they also came increasingly under attack from the Thatcher governments. Single payments (grants available to supplementary benefit claimants for such items as cookers or bedding), for example, generated growing concern within government about rising expenditure. Tony Newton, then a junior DHSS minister, claimed that '...the present torrent of claims could cause the breakdown of the entire social security system'.[15] As part of the reforms in social security, the single payments scheme was severely curtailed from 1986, and finally replaced with the social fund in 1988. 'Demand-led' rights to one-off grants had been abolished, to be replaced, in most instances, by discretionary loans, available from a cash-limited budget.[16]

Welfare rights work was undermined – and many felt it was now in retreat – having to fight harder and harder to retain fewer and fewer rights. This position was exacerbated by threats to the security of welfare rights workers themselves as a result of cuts in the funding of local agencies though local authority grant reductions, and the removal of forms of support for voluntary agencies through the Manpower Services Commission's Community Programme. Together, these developments constituted an assault on the welfare rights movement, forcing those involved to work out new strategies for the future of welfare rights work within the welfare state.[17]

Of course, the attack on welfare rights was in part a back-handed recognition of the serious threat it posed to the Thatcherite strategy. And, rather than demonstrating the obsolescence of public services, Thatcherism's attempts to replace state with market provision led to greater divisions, as has been discussed in Chapter 3. As we enter the 1990s, with the Citizen's Charter and emphasis on 'quality' in public services (see Chapters 8 and 9), a new agenda for welfare services is opening up. The opportunity exists for welfare rights to fight back against the challenge of the retreat from state welfare, and also the failings revealed in many of the old post-war institutions of public service. Indeed, perhaps welfare rights now has the chance to play a central role in renewing concern for the delivery, quality and performance of welfare over the next decade, making good the failures of the past.

Welfare rights and citizenship

This potential renewal of interest in welfare rights is likely to be linked to a renewal of concern with the much-debated concept of citizenship. As discussed in Chapter 7, citizenship is a widely used – and widely misused – concept which, in many cases, has operated to exclude people from welfare and cash payments, rather than securing their welfare rights. Both rights and citizenship were central to the thinking of influential supporters of the post-war welfare state. Marshall argued that the welfare state could provide members of society with social citizenship, to supplement the civil and legal citizenship which had been achieved in earlier times, and that rights to welfare would be central in realising such an objective.[18] In practice, however, many of the rights to welfare enshrined in the post-war welfare state – for example national insurance – provided only conditional rights to benefit and operated to exclude significant groups – married women and recent immigrants, to name but a few.

However, neither citizenship nor rights need be exclusionary concepts. In a reformulation of Marshall's third dimension of social citizenship to provide a right for everyone to share to the full in the social heritage, rights to welfare services for all could empower users, as citizens, to *demand* welfare services.[19] If enforceable rights were to replace the discretionary powers of bureaucrats and professionals, welfare rights could challenge the paternalism of many public services. Enforceable rights to public services *of a decent and measurable quality* would also challenge the private contract model of individual rights promoted by neo-liberals and the Thatcher governments of the 1980s, because welfare rights would not be conditional upon ability to pay in the market, and would be 'quality' rights, not rights to second-class or poor services.

The pursuit of welfare rights raises issues of resources. This has led some on the Right to argue that, unlike civil and political rights, welfare rights cannot be granted unconditionally because they would lead to an overload on public resources.[20] Plant, who is perhaps the most established supporter of citizenship rights, has questioned this presumption, arguing that civil and political rights also have commensurate resource obligations.[21] But, in rights-based welfare services, conditions of entitlement will be public and open to legal challenge, as arguably the distribution of support for welfare services should be, rather than, as it has been far too often in the past, subject to the professional judgement or bureaucratic discretion of state employees.

The question of obligation also raises the issue of whether the right to welfare should give rise to 'obligations' on the part of citizens who receive welfare services (see also Chapter 2). Plant argues that in principle reciprocity and contribution are essential features of any regime based upon citizenship.[22] However, as Lister discusses, the imposition of obligations in return for citizenship rights is a complex issue in which very sharp differences of both practice and principle can be confused.[23] For instance, supporters of the 'active citizen' model of obligation foresee a self-reliant citizenship as a basis for reducing the collective obligations of government. This is not a model which fits well with Plant's notion of citizenship as a basis for conferring universal social rights.

Thus, in principle, universal rights, including rights to state support, do need to be supported by obligations on all citizens to contribute to the society in which these rights are enjoyed. But current circumstances of increasing unemployment and inadequate training opportunities are likely to mean that obligations required in return for welfare rights would be tainted with punitive connotations of workfare and work-search, which operate in practice to exclude claimants from welfare rather than to extend it to them. Until broader reforms of employment opportunities and training provisions are taken up, conditional entitlements are unlikely to be a desirable feature of renewed welfare rights.

The renewal of interest in social citizenship and welfare rights in the 1990s is likely to receive further impetus from the increasing impact of European Community (EC) policy on its member states (see Chapter 5). EC discussion of the need for co-ordination and harmony in economic policy after 1992 has already begun to extend to proposals for harmonisation in social policies. Within the EC Charter of Fundamental Social Rights of Workers there is a focus on the notion of rights as a vehicle for achieving social policy objectives. The Charter also elaborates a broader emphasis on rights at work linked to rights to welfare (although a right to social assistance for non-workers has now also been introduced). In part, this reflects the labour market concerns of the EC; but it is also a recognition of the importance of relating social to economic policy planning if general improvements are to be achieved for everyone (see Chapter 9). This is demonstrated in particular by the right to a minimum wage, which was dropped on Mitterand's suggestion in 1989 in order – unsuccessfully as it turned out – to placate the UK.

Rights to welfare and rights at work are already better developed in a number of European countries than they are in the UK – for example, the minimum wage in France and health insurance rights in Germany. In this respect, the UK could learn much from its European neighbours – and is in any case likely to be required to improve its record as pressures towards harmonisation of rights throughout the EC increase. Not, of course, that this should be an excuse for waiting for change from Brussels. The EC 'subsidiarity' principle requires that steps to achieve co-ordinated provision should primarily be taken by national governments themselves (see Chapter 5 for a more detailed discussion).

Towards welfare rights

Rights to quality

The use of welfare rights to guarantee minimum standards demonstrates the important role that they could play in moves towards improved quality, and quality control, in welfare services. Issues of quality of service are being placed on the welfare agenda by all political perspectives in the 1990s, partly in recognition that market competition has not been successful in challenging or improving on the past failings of state welfare (see also Chapter 8). Of course, there has always been a mixture of public, voluntary, informal and private welfare services, and in the last decade the private sector in particular has been growing significantly. Within such 'welfare pluralism' there may be the fear therefore that, even where backed by rights, state services will come to occupy a residual and secondary role.

This is a real fear. Nevertheless, moves towards welfare rights, and particularly towards *rights to quality* in public, privatised, private and voluntary services, could operate to counteract such tendencies. Thus, rights are likely to be at the centre of the development of welfare in the 1990s, whoever wins the next election. It is important that such tendencies are encouraged and extended. Welfare rights can promote a much needed *certainty* in public welfare provision, to displace discretion and professional control. They can provide certainty in what users of services can expect, which can be publicised and supported through advice and advocacy; and they can provide certainty in what providers should deliver, which can be secured by independent enforcement through legal machinery.

By providing enforceable rights to minimum standards of welfare service across all sectors and for all users, welfare rights can challenge the threat that public services will become poor quality services. The rights basis would apply equally to all and would therefore be a major vehicle for equal standards. Plant argues that rights could be tied to performance indicators to ensure that quality services are provided.[24] In the informal and voluntary sectors in particular, however, rights for users must also be balanced against rights for providers and carers. (The right to move between sectors would also be of crucial importance here.)

User participation

One criticism of state services, articulated particularly by those on the Right, is that they have not shown themselves to be flexible in responding to the *differing* needs of individual consumers. This is also a criticism which could be levelled at welfare rights. Welfare rights should be a dynamic, not a static, feature of service provision; and changes to rights *can* be influenced by consumer demands, especially if such demands are incorporated, through user participation, into the administration and review of all services. However, Plant has suggested that flexibility can also be attained by giving customers, where possible, rights and choice in services, through the use of cash and cash surrogates (such as vouchers) which place more control in users' hands.[25] For instance, Hewitt, from the Institute for Public Policy Research, has proposed a voucher for childcare provision for the under-fives, to be used by parents in any of a range of approved facilities.[26]

However, user participation must also address the difficult issue of involving users in the determination and pursuit of welfare rights – in particular if we are to avoid the threat of the profes-sionalisation of welfare rights work itself, referred to above.[27] This will involve the mobilisation of users, many of whom will have little experience of practical participation in formal decision-making and policy development. This is no easy task, but it is one which is increasingly being recognised in policy circles.[28]

A rights-based approach

New priorities

The legislation and enforcement of rights are two different sides of a new future for welfare. The theory must also be backed up by practice; if rights are to be realised in welfare services, changes will be needed to embrace a rights-based approach to delivery and enforcement.

This will mean changes in the structure of state institutions – for example, the DSS, and now the Benefits Agency, will need to re-prioritise the delivery of rights. This will involve the development of rights-based (re-)training for all benefits workers. It will require the recruitment of welfare rights specialists into agencies to ensure internal policy development and accountability.[29] Commitment to the enforcement of welfare rights will also require stable financial support for agencies – especially in the community and voluntary sectors – working to secure rights through advice and advocacy work. This should also include support for new initiatives such as the Citizen Advocacy Schemes provided by organisations such as Age Concern, which are based upon encouraging members to act as advocates for one another in pursuing rights, thus avoiding the 'professionalism' which might be associated with use of specialist advisers. 'Bottom-up' initiatives such as these are also more likely to make the enforcement of welfare rights sensitive to the different needs and circumstances of different service users, such as ethnic minority groups who use English as a second language.[30]

Reducing means-testing

In social security, a renewed concern with rights to benefits must include a reappraisal of the growing dominance of means-testing within benefit provision. Means-tested benefits do not provide the best method of securing rights to income for claimants, as the high levels of non-take-up for all major means-tested benefits testify. A move towards welfare rights in social security should therefore build upon benefits such as child benefit, which do provide clear and readily enforceable rights without a means test (see also Chapter 9). Because of its universal nature, child benefit is readily available, and recognises, through social security provision, the investment that we all have individually and collectively in providing for future generations of citizens.

Social insurance

A move towards benefits based on more secure rights will also require a renewed commitment to, and a restructuring of, 'social insurance' benefits for adults. The positive aspect of insurance-based benefits is that they provide support as of right to *individuals* at times of need resulting from their exclusion from the labour market, thus avoiding the inefficiencies and the stigma of means-testing, and the enforced dependency of the family unit basis of means-tested benefits. However, in practice, current limitations on entitlement to insurance benefits – resulting from stringent contribution conditions – operate to exclude many individuals from receiving them; and the punitive measures imposed on unemployed claimants, in order to demonstrate their 'availability for work', impose unnecessarily harsh obligations on those seeking a right to state support.

Thus, a new model of rights-based social insurance needs to be developed to provide support for periods of non-employment for all, without recourse to individual contribution tests. Such a right to individual insurance benefits for those not in the labour market, together with the right to a statutory minimum wage for those in employment, could provide a new basis for rights to adequate support for all those currently experiencing poverty and having to rely upon inadequate means-tested support. These rights could also be extended to the growing numbers of part-time workers, through the payment of minimum wages together with the payment of insurance benefits to individuals, calculated on an hourly basis within a given working week.

Conclusion

Over the years CPAG has strongly supported many of the above developments in social security rights. *In principle*, through support for clearer social security rights, and *in practice,* through training, advice and advocacy work, CPAG has in fact been at the centre of the development of welfare rights in the UK over the last two decades. This is a position which must be both consolidated and expanded in the 1990s, as rights come to feature more and more centrally on the broader welfare agenda.

At great cost to those at the bottom of an increasingly unequal social order, and those excluded from the privileged contractual rights afforded by the private sector, the 1980s have demonstrated that the market alternative to public welfare cannot deliver quality services *for all.* However, as critics on both Right and Left now recognise, the paternalistic state institutions of the post-war welfare settlement have also failed to guarantee appropriate provision for their customers, especially those people who live in poverty or on low incomes. As we move into the 1990s, therefore, the right of all citizens to responsive and enforceable welfare services, however these are provided, must challenge these past failings of both state and market with a new movement towards real rights to quality welfare services.

Notes

1. The recommendations in the Beveridge report were based on the belief that social security should be perceived as a right, procured through insurance, rather than as a discretionary payment from the state, as was the case with most pre-war benefit provision: Sir W Beveridge, *Report on Social Insurance and Allied Services,* HMSO, 1942.

2. Marshall argued that social citizenship rights should be the basis of state welfare, to complement the civil and political citizenship rights developed in earlier eras: T H Marshall, *Citizenship and Social Class,* Cambridge University Press, 1952.

3. For further discussion see: S Ward (ed), *DHSS in Crisis: Social Security – Under Pressure and Under Review,* CPAG, 1985.

4. R Berthoud, S Benson and S Williams, *Standing Up for Claimants: Welfare Rights Work in Local Authorities,* PSI, 1986, p12.

5. See C Cannan, 'Welfare rights and wrongs', in R Bailey and M Brake (eds), *Radical Social Work,* Edward Arnold, 1975; and R Cohen and A Rushton, *Welfare Rights,* Heinemann Educational Books, 1982.

6. See P Alcock, 'Poverty, welfare and the local state', in P Lawless and C Raban (eds), *The Contemporary British City,* Harper & Row, 1986.

7. See London-Edinburgh Weekend Return Group, *In and Against the State,* Pluto Press, 1979.

8. R Cohen and A Rushton, *see* note 5; and T Prosser, *Test Cases for the Poor: Legal Techniques in the Politics of Social Welfare,* CPAG, 1983.

9. For instance, the Greater London Council claimed that their take-up campaign

work in the 1980s produced £10 million worth of extra benefits for Londoners; see P Alcock and J Shepherd, 'Take-up campaigns: fighting poverty through the post', *Critical Social Policy,* Issue 19, 1987.

10. For instance, Jackie Drake's successful challenge in the European Court of Justice to the exclusion of married and cohabiting women from entitlement to invalid care allowance, supported by CPAG; see R Smith, 'Lolly for the lollipop lady', *Poverty,* No 64, CPAG, 1986.

11. For instance, in 1989 the Central Council for Education and Training in Social Work published the report of its Curriculum Development Group advocating a rights-based perspective to social work education; J Stewart (ed), *Welfare Rights in Social Work Education,* CCETSW Paper 28.1, 1989.

12. See, for example, P Beresford and S Croft, *Whose Welfare? Private Care or Public Services,* Lewis Cohen Urban Studies Centre, Brighton Polytechnic, 1986.

13. *See* note 4.

14. The advice to replace discretionary payments with legal entitlements was contained in the report of a DHSS review team, and the Labour government did not act on it because of fears that such a reform would have resource implications at a time when attempts were being made to contain public expenditure; DHSS, *Social Assistance: A Review of the Supplementary Benefits Scheme in Great Britain,* HMSO, 1978.

15. *Hansard,* vol 102, col 444, 1986.

16. See G Craig (ed), *Your Flexible Friend: Voluntary Organisations, Claimants and the Social Fund,* Social Security Consortium, 1989.

17. P Alcock, J Shepherd, G Stewart and J Stewart, 'Welfare rights work into the 1990s – a changing agenda', *Journal of Social Policy,* Vol 20, No 1, 1991.

18. *See* note 2.

19. *See* note 2, p11.

20. N Barry, 'Markets, citizenship and the welfare state: some critical reflections', in R Plant and N Barry, *Citizenship and Rights in Thatcher's Britain: Two Views,* IEA Health and Welfare Unit, 1990.

21. For instance, see R Plant, *Citizenship, Rights and Socialism,* Fabian Society Pamphlet No 531, 1988.

22. *See* note 21, Chapter 4.

23. R Lister, *The Exclusive Society: Citizenship and the Poor,* CPAG Ltd, 1990, Chapter 1.

24. R Plant, 'Citizenship and rights', in R Plant and N Barry; *see* note 20.

25. *See* note 21, pp12-13.

26. P Hewitt, 'A way to cope with the world as it is', *Samizdat,* No 6, 1989, pp3-4.

27. *See* note 12.

28. R Lister, 'Working together against poverty', *Benefits,* Issue 2, October 1991.

29. For instance, see the discussion of the implications of developing welfare rights services within social service departments in G Fimister, *Welfare Rights Work in Social Services,* Macmillan, 1986.

30. For instance, see the work of local agencies in Islington, discussed in: Islington People's Rights, *English Speakers Only,* 1984.

7.

Forms of exclusion: citizenship, race and poverty

Paul Gordon

In an age of citizenship there are two sorts of non-citizens: those who have never been admitted, and those who have been exiled.

Sarah Benton[1]

...the great problem, the biggest problem of the next century – the problem of 'Other'.

Carlos Fuentes[2]

SINCE the mid-1980s, the idea of citizenship has seemed to dominate much of political discussion in the UK.[3] Yet such discourse, while recognising that citizenship in Britain has always had a very restricted meaning, has too often failed to recognise the ways in which citizenship has worked to exclude black people. This is true whether we consider citizenship in a strictly legal sense or in a wider political sense. In a legal sense, citizenship was and essentially still is a device for the administration of immigration control, an aspect of policy whose principal aim has been to keep as many black people as possible, whether Asians or Afro-Caribbeans, out of the country. In a political sense, many black people have, in practice, been effectively excluded from meaningful participation in political or civic life through the operation of racism. This includes the ways in which they have been excluded as a result of poverty, a condition which, as Ruth Lister has shown, undermines people's ability to fulfil their private and public obligations at the same time as effectively excluding them from the full rights of citizenship.[4] Any discussion of citizenship must take account of these forms of exclusion if it is not to perpetuate a myth of universality which is, in fact, a story of exclusion and particularity. It cannot ignore what citizenship has meant, *in practice*, for black people in Britain.

This chapter examines how black people have been excluded from legal citizenship through immigration and nationality legislation, and then at the informal exclusions which result from racism, including the impact of poverty on black people. Finally, it considers the propects for citizenship in the 'New Europe' now taking shape.

Citizens, subjects and immigrants

Until 1948, the primary distinction in British law was that between British subjects and aliens. Only British subjects had rights – they were free from immigration control, had the right to vote, to stand for Parliament, to join the Civil Service and to own a British ship. The British Nationality Act of that year – passed to take account of the fact that the dominions were creating their own citizenships – created a new status of Citizen of the UK and Colonies, which was to be shared by the people of the UK and the peoples of the dependencies. All would continue to be British subjects by virtue of being citizens of a Commonwealth country.[5]

Citizens of the United Kingdom and Colonies (CUKCs), regardless of whether they came from the UK or the colonies, shared a common status. But a process of differentiation and exclusion soon began. In the late 1940s and early 1950s, concern at the numbers of black people migrating to Britain led first to informal attempts to curtail rights to immigration and then, in the 1960s, to formal controls through legislation. This is not the place to rehearse the detail and the injustices of this legislation. Suffice to say that, beginning with the Commonwealth Immigrants Act 1962, immigration legislation and the immigration rules made under it stripped black CUKCs of the primary right associated with their citizenship – their right of abode in Britain. It became increasingly difficult for black CUKCs to come to Britain, while those who did gain entry became ever more liable to deportation or removal. By the mid-1970s, some CUKCs, mainly white, had rights of abode and settlement in the UK, while others, mainly black, had no such rights. The status was common in name, but not in content.

By this time also there were no fewer than five categories of people for the purposes of immigration control and it was these categories which, generally speaking, became translated into the five categories of citizen introduced by the 1981 British Nationality Act. The Act also created, for the first time in history, a category of British citizen. Only they, along with some long-settled Commonwealth citizens, now have the right of abode in the UK, which remains the only right attached to citizenship.

Whatever the exact form of words used, over two decades from 1962 to 1981 British citizenship – what it meant to belong to Britain – was redefined so as to exclude a great many black people who had not long before been considered British through their status as Citizens of the UK and Colonies. Citizenship, at least in this legal sense, has itself therefore been a form of exclusion for many black people. But such legal definition is not the only, or even the main, form of exclusion from citizenship.

Forms of exclusion

Just as important as formal exclusion from legal citizenship are the ways in which people who are citizens are, in practice, excluded from meaningful participation in civic life. Sarah Benton has argued that this has been true, for example, of women for whom the concepts of rights and of citizenship, of 'liberty, equality and *fraternity*', were of little use in their struggles against male domination and for political, economic and social equality. Indeed, Benton argues, there is a real sense in which men and women have met as enemies, as limitations on one another's freedoms.[6]

So, too, as a number of CPAG publications have shown, citizenship, in the sense of meaningful participation in civic life, requires certain minimal levels of resources, including time and material wealth.[7] The woman who has an elderly or sick relative to care for, or the parent who must look after children, participate in civic life on terms quite different from those who either have no such responsibilities, or who have money to pay others to do things to give them free time. In the same way, the poor are excluded in a number of ways – the enforcement of rights to welfare provision can be impossible without the resources to obtain legal advice or assistance; the homeless are readily disenfranchised, as were those who refused to enter the electoral roll in case this was used to compile the poll tax register. Poverty, as Peter Golding put it, 'is most comprehensively understood as a condition of partial citizenship', excluding the poor not just from their legal citizenship rights but also from the opportunities offered by a society.[8] Furthermore, as Bea Campbell notes, those who are poor are also excluded from the politics necessary to challenge their condition:

> Like pleasure, politics costs money. The poor are collectively starved of political resources and support... The very fact of unemployment cuts the wageless off from the resources of the waged working class and its labour movement. They aren't just individually unequal, they have unequal access to the resources of organisations... Time the unemployed have got, money they haven't.[9]

Black people, too, can be excluded from meaningful participation as citizens through the operation of a racism which restricts choices and opportunities. Just as poverty excludes white poor people, so does it affect more and more black people as poverty becomes increasingly racialised. As a result of government economic policies and global recession, an increasing proportion of black people has become poor. Although few data are available specifically on ethnicity and poverty – the official data sources for estimating poverty provide no racial breakdown – some facts are clear. The proportion of black people out of work is, roughly speaking, twice that of white people; those in work are likely to be earning less than their white counterparts (up to 20 per cent less according to one recent survey);[10] black households, which tend to be larger than those of whites, are more likely to be situated in poorer areas, and were particularly badly hit by the poll tax;[11] and the age profile and family structures of black people make them more vulnerable to poverty.[12]

Such poverty affects black people as it does white; but it can also affect some black people in ways that are further-reaching. For instance, the right of settled immigrants to be joined here by their families from abroad depends on their ability to maintain and accommodate them; this was the result of the 1988 Immigration Act which withdrew from Commonwealth citizens settled here before 1973 (when the 1971 Immigration Act came into force) their automatic right to be joined here by their spouses and dependants. Now such people are debarred from having 'recourse to public funds'. In other words, people who have lived here for years, and who have worked and paid taxes here, are now allowed to be joined by their families from abroad only on condition that they do not claim benefits for them and can provide them with accommodation. Not only are these requirements not imposed on other people lawfully settled here – European Community (EC) citizens, for instance, are entitled to bring in an extended range of relatives free of any such conditions – but they represent a breach of an undertaking in the 1971 Immigration Act which promised that the rights of those already settled in the country would not be adversely affected. Thus these requirements constituted a further limitation of black people's citizenship.

Poverty also makes it more difficult for people who are not already British citizens to acquire such status. The British Nationality Act of 1981 took away the automatic right of settled Commonwealth citizens to register as British citizens if they had not exercised this by the end of 1987, thus making many more people liable to the discretionary and more expensive process of naturalisation. At the same time, the cost of acquiring citizenship has also increased. Naturalisation now costs up to £170 for each person applying, and fees must be paid in advance, even though applications take up to three years to be processed. Those whose applications are rejected are subject to a punitive non-refundable deposit of £135 in the case of a full-fee naturalisation. A recommendation by the Parliamentary Home Affairs Committee in 1983, that those on benefit pay no fee at all and that there be a single fee for a family application, was rejected out of hand by the government.

Black people seeking welfare benefits also encounter barriers additional to those faced by claimants in general. Over the years entitlement to welfare benefits has become increasingly tied to immigration status, thus creating a class of black people who are lawfully resident in the country – people who have been sponsored on condition that they do not have recourse to public funds, fiancé(e)s similarly barred until they have married – but who have fewer rights than others. This affects all black people, not just those who are, in fact, subject to restrictions. After all, how is a black person who is covered by the rules to be distinguished from one who is not? Hence the widespread questioning of black people about their immigration status, even those born or long-settled here; hence, too, the frequent wrongful refusal of benefits through misunderstanding and misapplication of the rules. So, too, the absence of information and advice in minority languages is an effective barrier to the exercise of rights by people whose first language is not English. All this has been documented by various reports which suggest that black people are indeed 'second-class claimants'.[13]

But the exclusion of black people from citizenship runs deeper than the barriers to benefits and the impact of poverty. It is to be found in the effects of a whole range of policies and laws, of commissions and omissions, whose effect, intended or not, is to exclude black people from the rights and opportunities available to others. These include economic policies which lead to a black unemployment rate twice that of white people and to the concentration of black workers in lower-paid jobs; health policies which pay insufficient regard to the specific health problems of black people; and housing policies which result in the concentration of black families in the worst public housing, while black homeless people are, out of proportion to their numbers in the population, confined to squalid bed and breakfast accommodation. Most important of all, the very freedom to walk the streets, to go about one's business, is curtailed for many black people by the threat and reality of racist violence.[14]

This exclusion takes place also at the level of ideas and identities through a denial of cultural, religious and other difference. 'Labour says he's black. We say he's British', ran a Conservative Party advertisement for the 1983 general election, while six years later, in the context of *The Satanic Verses* controversy, a Conservative Home Secretary told British Muslims that they should embrace British ways and integrate more into British society. The message in both cases was clear: it is not possible to be both – black and British, Muslim and British – and there is a choice to be made.

When we address the relationship between race and citizenship, we see a process in which black people have been stripped of rights through immigration legislation – the right to enter the UK, the right to settle here, to be joined by families - and that citizenship, as defined and employed, was a means of doing this. Taking a broader view of citizenship, we see how black people who are British citizens or lawfully settled here are affected by policies which have a discriminatory impact, and how their citizenship rights and status are therefore limited.

Citizenship and the new Europe

The 'new Europe' coming into being as a result of the UK's increasing integration into the EC, the advent of the Single European Market to be achieved by the end of 1992 and greater political and economic cooperation within continental Europe as a whole, will have profound implications for the question of citizenship in Britain. Many European countries have histories of citizenship, of written constitutions, defined rights and responsibilities, and, above all, *cultures* of citizenship, while the democratic movements in the countries of the former Soviet bloc have adopted ideas of citizenship and civil society as essential components of their anti-authoritarian politics. Yet the new Europe coming into being, whether as a result of the Single European Market and the expansion of the European Community, or through the collapse of the Communist east, is a Europe built on exclusion, on citizenship for some but not all.

As with national citizenship, this exclusion takes a number of forms. There is, in the European Community, the exclusion from full citizenship of the 'thirteenth state' of migrants and refugees, legal and illegal, whose labour is necessary to run the service industries, clean the streets and do the rest of the dirty work indigenous workers do not want to do. Numbering anything from 8 to 12 million people, they not only do not enjoy the rights of EC migrants – to freedom of movement, family unity and so on – but are (with a few exceptions) excluded from citizenship and civic life in the countries in which they live, work and pay taxes, with no right to vote, to seek employment in the public sector, or even, in some countries, to form their own associations. So, too, refugees and asylum-seekers from the Third World are already being excluded through increasingly restrictive asylum laws and procedures by both individual states and the EC as a whole, while even short-term visitors, also from the Third World, will be increasingly liable to exclusion through the operation of a common immigration and visa policy.

Nor will the much-vaunted Single European Market, with its greatly reduced barriers to the free movement of capital, goods and people, and its promise to extend opportunities within the twelve countries of the European Community, be truly open even to those who are Community citizens. While it will be easier for individuals to travel to another country to work, to open or expand a business, or to study, exclusions will apply. Those who do not have material resources will be less equal than those who do. It is a lot easier, for example, for someone with resources to travel abroad to seek work, and those with educational or other formal qualifications are likely to find the new Europe more congenial than those without. And, in a culture of racism, those who are black, or perceived as 'not white', are likely to find their 'freedom of movement' and 'right of establishment' limited by racism and discrimination in countries, in a culture, to which they may formally belong, but from which they are excluded. (It is worth noting here that the European Community's Charter of Fundamental Social Rights of Workers, much-vaunted as inaugurating a new era of rights for workers, had nothing to say about the right not to be discriminated against because of one's colour or ethnic origin, and even now in its present form only includes a general statement in its preamble to this effect.)

Those who are not nationals of EC countries, people who include refugees and asylum-seekers, migrant workers and settled residents who hold a non-EC nationality – the Jamaican or Sri Lankan national who has lived in Britain for twenty years, the Turkish worker who has been living in Germany for seven years, the South African asylum-seeker in Denmark – none of these will share in the new opportunities promised by the Single European Market. And neither will the Single European Market be open to thousands of people in Britain, mostly black, who are excluded from EC rights of freedom of movement because they are not British citizens, even though they have all the other rights of citizenship and are permanently settled here.[15]

But there is another form of exclusion. An exclusion at the level of ideas, an exclusion of those who do not conform to the image that the new Europe has of itself. This image holds, implicitly if not always explicitly, that to be European is to be white, Christian and holding to a Eurocentric view of the world, and that to be other than this is to be 'Other', to be outside. It is to be one of 'the barbarian people', as a Belgian Interior Minister put it, 'such as Arabs, Moroccans, Yugoslavs and Turks, people who come from far afield and have nothing in common with our civilisation',[16] or one of those people who, as Margaret Thatcher put it when Prime Minister, come from a world which was not only 'explored and colonised' but 'civilised' by Europeans in an 'extraordinary tale of talent, skill and courage',[17] or, again, one of the 'noisy and smelly foreigners' described recently by former French Prime Minister Jacques Chirac.[18] Those who do not see themselves in such descriptions will find that Europe has little place for them; indeed they are already doing so as waves of racist murders and assaults occur across Europe, from the Atlantic coast to the Ural mountains.

Citizenship and the future

As mentioned earlier, the concept of citizenship has come to dominate much of British political discourse. The Claim of Right for Scotland and the Scottish Constitutional Convention, Charter 88, Charter 90 for Asians, the Bill of Rights published by the left-inclined think tank, the Institute for Public Policy Research – all testify to this new-found constitutionalism. For their part, the political parties too have taken up the cause of citizenship, moulding it to fit their own political projects. The Conservatives have previously espoused the concept of the 'active citizen', who gives time or money in some form of public service. The Labour Party, although opposed to a Bill of Rights as such, has expressed support for tougher legislation against discrimination and in support of equal opportunities based on a positive declaration that everyone has the right to be treated equally without any differentiation on the grounds of sex or race.[19] The (Social and) Liberal Democrats support a Bill of Rights and the eventual adoption of a written constitution,[20] while the Green Party has promulgated a Charter for Citizens' Power, in order to establish genuine citizen-centred government.[21]

The major problem with all the movements for constitutional reform and an extension of rights is their limited concept of change. Regardless of their merits or de-merits, changes such as those proposed would leave many categories of people excluded from meaningful citizenship in the sense of the ability to participate fully in civil and political life. Thus, for example, Michael Rustin has criticised Charter 88 for opting for a definition of citizenship concerned almost exclusively with civil and political rights and 'scarcely at all' with the social and economic rights of citizens.[22]

If rights are to be guaranteed and genuine citizenship ensured, constitutional reform is certainly necessary, but it is not sufficient. An uncritical acceptance of the concept of 'citizenship' will not do either. The black experience of citizenship, as with the experience of women and poor people (with which it interacts), reveals the exclusionary nature of citizenship. In this area, as in so many others, the black experience provides one of the 'most important keys, not into the margins of society, but right into its dynamic centre'.[23] In other words, it shows that citizenship is itself an exclusionary concept: that to define some people as citizens is, in precisely the same move and at precisely the same time, to define others as not-citizens. To include is, by definition, also to exclude. The challenge facing the protagonists of citizenship and constitutionalism is to go beyond formal legal rights to recognise a basic right of all people to participate meaningfully in the civic and political life of the society in which they live, regardless of their status, gender or ethnic or racial origins. What is needed is a genuinely pluralist, more embracing form of citizenship, which is not tolerant of difference, for that implies a superiority and resignation on the part of the tolerant, but which welcomes it as a fact of our contemporary life.

As far as racial or ethnic minorities are concerned, the 'new Europe' now coming into being will be host to significant numbers of non-European people whether it likes it or not. 'The city of the 21st century', the Mexican writer Carlos Fuentes says, 'promises to be the city of the encounter with "the other" – a woman, a man, a child from another race, another culture, who enriches himself among us at the same time as he enriches the rest of us – as long as we assimilate the extraneous and accept his cultural identity.' The main actor in this 'universality', Fuentes goes on, is the migrant worker who arrives in our cities defying our prejudices, challenging us to say whether cultural diversity can co-exist with social justice. Fuentes concludes: 'The universality that might bring us together is this: history has not finished and the protagonists are ourselves and the others. Between the two of us we may create the 21st century's city, a multiracial and multicultural city which will be the greatest achievement of instant communications, economic integration and cultural variety.'[24]

Fuentes' use of the word 'may' in this passage makes it clear that there is a choice; we may create the city of the future, or we may not. The choice facing the protagonists of citizenship is of continuing with a form of exclusion or of creating a meaningful concept which can embrace this 'Other' in all its various forms. This requires a recognition of the changed nature of Europe and individual European societies. Paradoxically, 1992, with all its attendant racist thinking and attitudes of exclusion, also offers the possibility of a genuinely multicultural, multiracial society. 1992 is not just the year of the Single European Market; it is also the quincentennial of the so-called discovery of the Americas, an occasion, no doubt, for yet more celebration of the supposed European achievement. Yet 1992 also presents an opportunity to deconstruct the false image that Europe has of itself, an opportunity to begin to create a new image which recognises Europe's true history of colonialism, imperialism and exploitation, and recognises too the contribution of non-Europeans to the building of Europe, from the Moors to today's 'thirteen state' of immigrants, migrants and refugees.

Notes

1. S Benton, 'Gender, sexuality and citizenship', in G Andrews (ed), *Citizenship,* Lawrence and Wishart, 1991.
2. 'Too soon to hail capitalism's triumph', *The Guardian,* 27 December 1990.
3. See R Lister, *The Exclusive Society: Citizenship and the Poor,* CPAG Ltd, 1990, for a review of the meanings and uses of the concept.
4. *See* note 3.
5. For a history of the development of citizenship and nationality law see A Dummett and A Nicol, *Subjects, Citizens, Aliens and Others: Nationality and Immigration Law,* Weidenfeld and Nicholson, 1990.
6. *See* note 1.
7. See, for example, P Golding (ed), *Excluding the Poor,* CPAG Ltd, 1986.
8. *See* note 7, pxi.
9. B Campbell, *Wigan Pier Revisited,* Virago, 1984, p18.
10. K B Duffy and I C Lincoln, *Earnings and Ethnicity,* Leicester City Council, 1990.
11. *Black People, Ethnic Minorities and the Poll Tax,* Association of London Authorities, 1988, summarised in *Race and Immigration,* No 214, April 1988.
12. C Oppenheim, *Poverty: The Facts,* CPAG Ltd, 1990.
13. See, for instance, National Association of Citizens' Advice Bureaux, *Barriers to Benefit: Black Claimants and Social Security,* NACAB, 1991; S Becker and R Silburn, *The New Poor Clients: Poverty, Social Work and the Social Fund,* Community Care/Benefits Research Unit, 1990; and P Gordon and A Newnham, *Passport to Benefits? Racism and Social Security,* CPAG and Runnymede Trust, 1985.
14. For a review of the impact of government policies on black people see P Gordon, *Citizenship for Some: Race and Government Policy 1979-89,* Runnymede Trust, 1989.
15. The definition of British national used for European Community purposes includes British citizens but also some British Dependent Territories Citizens (Gibraltarians) and some others, but not Commonwealth citizens (who remain British subjects) or other British passport-holders.
16. Quoted in *The Guardian,* 27 December 1988.
17. Rt Hon. Margaret Thatcher MP, Speech to College of Europe, Bruges, quoted in the *Daily Telegraph,* 22 September 1988.
18. Quoted in *The Times,* 21 June 1991.
19. *The Charter of Rights,* Labour Party, 1991.
20. *Partners for Freedom and Justice,* Social and Liberal Democrats, 1989.
21. *Charter for Citizens' Power,* Green Party Campaigns Department, 1991.
22. M Rustin, 'Whose rights of citizenship?', in G Andrews (ed), *Citizenship,* Lawrence and Wishart, 1991, p229. See also S Sedley: 'Charter 88: rights and wrongs', in the same volume.

23.   S Hall, 'Teaching race', *Multi-racial Education*, Vol 9, No 1, 1980.
24.   *See* note 2.

8.
A window of opportunity?

Fran Bennett

THIS chapter looks at the political starting-point for anti-poverty policies for the 1990s. What are the major political parties offering people in poverty in the run-up to, and beyond, the general election? The challenge to the parties is daunting, for two key reasons.

First, the numbers affected. The Social Security Select Committee's recent report showed that, in 1988 (latest figures available), 11.8 million people, or nearly 22 per cent of the population, were living in poverty (defined as below half average income after meeting housing costs).[1] As Chapter 3 shows, this total included 3 million children, or 25 per cent of all children in Great Britain. The poorest tenth of households had only paltry real increases in their income after housing costs between 1979 and 1988: 2 per cent, compared with 33.5 per cent for the population as a whole – although even these figures have been disputed in the increasingly political, and technical, debates that surround such data.

Second, the prospects for low-income families in the future. Unemployment is on the rise again, with some commentators forecasting an increase to 3 million people before the end of 1992. The character of the current recession, with its impact on services as well as manufacturing industry, suggests that the 'second earners'' (women's) part-time jobs, which must have kept thousands of families out of poverty in the 1980s, may be more at risk this time round. And, as we are reminded in Chapter 5, the increasing importance of factors *outside* the control of governments will influence the profile of poverty in the decade to come.

Chapter 2 warns of the danger of exaggerating the shift in priorities and policies represented by a change of prime minister. *The Times* identifies the new spirit as indicative more of a move towards consensus than away from Thatcherism as such:

...now both main parties salute opportunity, both embrace the entre-
preneur and both are concerned with wealth creation.[2]

And yet, there *is* a new spirit abroad, according to a concerted chorus
of commentators.[3] 'Fairness' is back on the public agenda; the word
'society' is heard regularly in politicians' speeches.

So what implications does this 'new politics' have for people in
poverty? The analysis which follows is based on the most up-to-date
published documents, and speeches by political leaders, of the three
main parties in Parliament.

Current Conservative concerns

Most lists of significant policy changes that have been drawn up since
John Major became prime minister in November 1990 have included
the increases in, and promised indexation of, child benefit; the
decision to make cold weather payments to claimants automatic in
future; and above all the abandonment of the poll tax. Thus, the main
indicators of a move away from Thatcherism tend to be clustered in
particular in CPAG's areas of concern – benefit payments, family
incomes and fairness in taxation. Not mentioned so often, but also
symbolic of a change of approach, are the withdrawal of higher-rate
mortgage interest tax relief, the freezing of the married couple's
allowance and the imposition of employers' national insurance
contributions on company cars – all steps taken in the 1991 Budget
which reduced the relative advantage enjoyed by certain more
privileged groups.

There has also been a more general, deliberate attempt to
emphasise the importance of social policy as we emerge from the
1980s. Chris Patten MP, Chairman of the Conservative Party, has
stated:

> Just as we won the argument on the economy in the 1980s, so I am
> absolutely convinced we can win the argument on social policy in the
> 1990s.[4]

Two other ministers have chosen to make social policy issues –
particularly the level and framework of benefits for the poor – the
major topic of their recent interventions in public debate.[5]

Prime Minister John Major's personal preference for a style of
consultation and consensus over conflict and confrontation has also

meant a palpably different attitude to the concerns and role of groups such as CPAG.[6] And the words used by John Major to set out his goals for the future seem to demonstrate a change of substance too. The Prime Minister twice described his vision of the society he would like to create as one that was 'at ease with itself'.[7] He called for the country to 'make the changes necessary to provide a better quality of life for *all* our citizens' [our emphasis];[8] and in the House of Commons, he said:

> Everyone is entitled to dignity and pride. The government's policies will endeavour to ensure that they can attain them.[9]

But how would these noble words be translated into policies for the rest of the 1990s? And what would they mean for low-income families?

First must be the new stress on 'opportunities'.[10] John Major has talked variously of 'choice', the 'chance to move to a better life' and a 'wider and deeper series of opportunities'.[11] But the precise content of the measures he would employ to bring about this desirable state of affairs is more difficult to discern. It does appear to be prejudiced from the start by an allegiance to the inherently circumscribed principle of ownership. 'No principle is more crucial than what I call the "right to own",' said John Major in the summer – referring, in particular, to a home, shares and pensions. Those who can benefit from the 'opportunities' offered by tax relief on mortgage interest and private pension provision will, it appears, continue to do so – thus effectively blocking off one major route for the government to create a fairer distribution of resources and hence wider opportunities for all.

Neither does the 'opportunity society' seem to be defined by an all-out attack on unemployment, to give more people the chance to start their ascent up the ladder. The Chancellor's remark that unemployment and the recession are a 'price well worth paying' for the reduction of inflation hardly suggests that reducing unemployment will be this government's priority.[12]

And yet this should be a high priority of any government determined to tackle poverty and increase opportunities, for two reasons in particular. Firstly, as Bradshaw writes, 'a child-centred economic policy is one that gives priority to reducing unemployment'; unemployment seriously blights children's life chances, health and happiness. Secondly, as Piachaud has argued:

> It may in theory be possible to maximise production and then consider its redistribution... Political experience suggests that prosperous producers will limit how much is redistributed to the non-producers. Therefore finding ways to enable as many as possible to be paid as producers is crucial for the reduction of poverty.[13]

In other words, the whole burden of redistribution cannot be put on those second-tier mechanisms, taxation and social security. Some adjustments *must* also be made to the distribution of original income, in particular through the expansion of job opportunities.

The government has argued, of course, that one way at least to avoid a decrease in job opportunities is to resist any further regulation of the labour market, which puts additional burdens on employers. Hence its vehement opposition to the European Community's (EC) new Social Charter (which relates largely to workers' rights), and its virulent denunciation of the Labour Party's plans for a national statutory minimum wage. Indeed, there have been strong hints that a new Conservative government would take this attitude to its logical conclusion, by abolishing the wages councils which currently set minimum pay rates for some of the lowest-paid workers.[14] Some argue that it is better to get any kind of job than none at all. But, in fact, recent research demonstrates that many unemployed people go in and out of the 'peripheral' labour market between bouts of unemployment, and therefore find that having a job is not always a secure step on the way out of poverty.[15]

Instead, the government plans to expand significantly the means-tested supplementation of earnings. From April 1992, with the qualifying hours for family credit being reduced from 24 to 16, even more families will be eligible, particularly lone-parent families. Simultaneously, the disability working allowance will be introduced – a means-tested top-up for low-paid workers with disabilities, with the same 16-hour qualifying limit and a similar structure to family credit.

However, there are inevitable contradictions for a government dedicated to 'opportunity for all' in pursuing such a policy. Means-tested benefits put an effective ceiling on aspirations, rather than providing a floor on which people can build by their own efforts, because they are withdrawn as other income increases (see also Chapter 6). The government has yet to come to terms with the problem that many people still see family credit, for example, as a 'hand-out', not a 'hand-up'.[16] A concentration on means-tested benefits also contradicts the government's desire to encourage personal savings for similar reasons.

There has been some disagreement over how far the new Cabinet's aim of 'quality in public services' represents a sea-change from Thatcherism. On the one hand, the government has made clear that it will continue its drive for 'more privatisation, more competition, contracting-out and less government intervention and regulation'.[17] On the other hand, Chris Patten's goal of raising public sector standards so high that the private sector will not be an automatic choice for the better off,[18] and John Major's linking of the Citizen's Charter with those – 'too many' – who had not yet felt the benefit of Conservative changes,[19] suggested an implicit rejection of a 'residual welfare state' and an explicit commitment to the public sector. Moreover, the typical individual envisaged as benefiting from the 'Citizen's Charter' – a citizen and a consumer – is a very different animal from the 'active citizen' of the later Thatcher years, prosperous and with time to spare for charity.[20]

Some problems with the Citizen's Charter[21] have already been identified. First is the fluidity of the concept itself. Everyone lays claim to it – including all three main political parties and, it appears, the major think-tanks too.

Second is the difficulty inherent in attempting to apply a Citizen's Charter to the social security system. While the Prime Minister was prepared to include 'benefit claimants' in his list of those – 'patients, passengers, parents, pupils, benefit claimants' – who should be able to know what standard of public service they can expect,[22] the social security section of the Citizen's Charter occupies less than two pages out of 51. The benefits system is perhaps the public service most in need of a consumer-oriented improvement in standards – but those parts offering the poorest service are precisely the benefits serving the poorest, and thus the ones least likely to attract public pressure for a better deal. And the new chief executive of the Benefits Agency, Michael Bichard, has already complained to MPs that the rise in unemployment is prejudicing performance standards in benefits delivery by his staff.[23]

Third, the government refuses to acknowledge either that the Charter itself would have significant costs if it were to work well, or that public services require more money regardless of its implementation.[24] Perhaps the most important of these from CPAG's perspective is childcare provision. Redress for dissatisfied customers is of no value to those who have no access to the service in the first place. The Citizen's Charter does *not* state that parents will be able to demand sufficient state-funded childcare places in their area to meet demand. And it says nothing about ending the exclusion of poor people from public services which results from increased charges for their use.

However, the debate about the Citizen's Charter may in the longer term contribute to a reversal of what Ruth Lister has called the 'revolution of reducing expectations' of social provision in the 1980s.[25] It is not clear whether this is something which the government realises. When the Prime Minister says that benefit claimants 'must know where they stand and what service they have a right to expect',[26] the uncertainties, inconsistencies and sheer random cruelties of the social fund stand out in sharp and ironic relief. The wider implications of the Citizen's Charter may potentially be far from conservative.

CPAG welcomed the 1991 Budget announcement committing the government not only to increasing child benefit from October 1991 but also to index-linking it in April 1992 and subsequent years. This is good news for all families and puts an end to the uncertainty about the government's intentions on child benefit even before publication of the Conservative manifesto, as CPAG had requested. But question marks remain. In particular, the index-linking commitment relates to the overall amount spent on child benefit, rather than to the individual benefit rates. While this does mean that the new structure for child benefit, with its bonus for the eldest eligible child in a family, will not be set in concrete, it also implies that the government could, for example, increase the rate for other children by more than inflation but reduce the level of the eldest child's payment in real terms. Since child benefit still falls short of its real level in 1987 by 30 pence per week for the eldest child and £2.05 for subsequent children (and should be £10 per child per week to maintain its real level before the cut in 1985), any such robbing Peter to pay Paul cannot be acceptable. CPAG believes that at a minimum the cuts in child benefit should be made good; that it should be index-linked for all children; and that there should then be a public debate about the most sensible structure for child support in the future. (This should of course include a re-examination of the balance between private and public support for children – which the government has tilted much further in the direction of private support through its new maintenance proposals.)

At present, the major tax change on the horizon appears to be the introduction of the council tax to replace the poll tax in 1993/94. From CPAG's point of view, a crucial change is the introduction of 100 per cent rebates for those on the lowest incomes, replacing the minimum contribution of 20 per cent of the poll tax. But equally, CPAG is very concerned that the government may seek to recover the 'compensation' given in benefits for the 20 per cent contribution – and that it seems at present that 100 per cent rebates will not be introduced in the remaining year and more of the poll tax. The council tax itself is a return to a property tax of sorts, but retaining a personal element in the form of the discount for single people.[27] It is likely to perpetuate the pressure on local authority services and tax levels, because of the low percentage of local tax raised at local level and because universal capping will be retained. It has also been criticised for not being progressive enough, by Tory MPs amongst others; the introduction of an eighth band, to cover properties of very high value (announced on 23 July 1991), modifies this structure only minimally.

The possibility that the income tax system will be made even less progressive by the reduction of the basic rate from 25 per cent, perhaps down to 20 per cent, cannot be discounted – although it appears that this is now a 'medium-term' ambition. Offsetting moves, to increase revenue from other sources such as indirect taxation, or to reduce public spending levels, would probably be needed.

The integration of the tax and social security systems has also been floated as a possible manifesto item, even though it was specifically rejected in a Green Paper by the government in 1986.[28] As Joe Rogaly points out, any such move would not mean the introduction of a non-means-tested income as of right for all.[29] Instead, it would be likely to move in the direction of a 'negative income tax' – the logical conclusion of a philosophy which sees social security benefits primarily as a relief and rescue mechanism for the few, rather than as a means of achieving collective security for all. Despite the change in ethos under John Major, it is unlikely that a new Conservative government would transform the politics of poverty relief for the casualties of the growing divisions throughout society that have characterised the last decade.

There may be a new spirit abroad which puts 'fairness' and the quality of public services higher up the agenda; but an article by John Biffen MP in *The Times* promoted a view which, if it is indicative of a new Conservative government's attitudes, will ensure that social provision is still subordinated to market demands:

> Free enterprise is the dynamo of wealth creation, and social welfare
> reconciles the public to the inequalities and penalties of failure
> inherent in a free market.[30]

Labour's plans

*In 1987 the Tories offered the politics of prosperity. We offered the
politics of compassion – people chose prosperity. This time we offer
both.*[31]

It is easier in some ways to analyse the Labour Party's programme for
government, because instead of having to read into the rhetoric of
ministerial speeches we can read about Labour's policies in a series
of pre-manifesto documents. The latest is *Opportunity Britain*,[32]
published in April 1991. It presents a policy package focused on
'pathways out of poverty', in particular for pensioners, people with
disabilities and families with children, as part of its action plan for the
future. The programme as a whole has been carefully developed since
1987, and results from a comprehensive policy review.

   The only two unequivocal commitments to increases in public
expenditure are to raise retirement pensions by £5 (for single people)
and £8 (for couples) per week, and to increase child benefit to make
good the loss in its value since 1987, with index-linking thereafter.
But the document also includes positive plans to introduce a minimum
wage – initially at half median male earnings, rising to two-thirds
over time; to make some minor improvements to income support
(including a premium for the long-term unemployed); and to introduce
a 'new social insurance scheme', which stresses qualification by
'category' of claimant rather than by contribution conditions (see
Chapter 6). There are plans for a new disability benefit made up of
two parts which would meet the extra costs of living with a disability,
and help those who either cannot work or can only work part of the
week. Pending a study of carers' needs, invalid care allowance would
be increased and entitlement would be extended more widely.
Labour would immediately convert all social fund loans into grants
and restore the right of appeal; it would then 'reassess' the social fund
'with the aim of ensuring that people receiving benefit obtain
payments for essential items ... which cannot be met from the weekly

allowance' – through discretionary payments for emergencies as well as a means of meeting regular needs. Taxation changes, in part to pay for the child benefit and pension pledges, include the abolition of the upper earnings limit on national insurance contributions for employees and raising the higher rate of income tax from 40 to 50 per cent. Couples could split the married couple's tax allowance between them. It would continue to be frozen, to provide money to raise child benefit and other support for families.

The emphasis on 'pathways out of poverty' is very welcome, suggesting a more ambitious programme than the mere maintenance of claimants on slightly more generous means-tested benefits. But the Labour Party has nonetheless found it difficult to shake off a more limited view of the purpose of social security and other anti-poverty strategies. Spokespersons persist in highlighting the role of child benefit as being 'the relief of poverty', for example, whereas its primary function is in fact to equalise the tax position of those with and those without children.[33] There is perhaps still not enough emphasis on the *prevention* of poverty as a policy goal, although, in practice, improvements to non-means-tested benefits and childcare provision would help to achieve this.

Labour's vulnerability to accusations that it is not helping 'the poorest' may explain this constant reversion to a traditional language of 'social provision [being] a matter of not being selfish' – Neal Ascherson's criticism of previous Labour programmes.[34] It has resulted in some modifications to policy which confuse Labour's policy goals. Labour's shadow Budget in 1991 was criticised by the government for not including increases in income support and family credit; it claimed that the poorest families would therefore not benefit from Labour's proposed child benefit increase. *Opportunity Britain*, however, includes the pledge that those on means-tested benefits will get the same increase as those only in receipt of child benefit when the loss since 1987 is made good. This is an unfortunate step, as it appears to fall into the trap of confusing help for all families with help for the worst-off.[35] There is, of course, a case for increasing the rates of income support (and hence family credit) for those with children – but not for confusing this with the quite separate case for restoring the real level of child benefit for all families. Both are essential; the arguments for each are distinct.

The Labour programme fails to include any proposal to improve significantly the level and duration of non-means-tested benefits for the unemployed and there is an obvious need for more detailed thought about the development of the new social insurance scheme. Potentially the use of conditions of entitlement, rather than a contribution record, is an exciting and radical move (see also Chapter 6). But CPAG knows from experience the complexities involved in thinking through questions of benefit entitlement for part-time workers, the relationship with earnings-relation and occupational benefits and in particular the creation of a constituency of support for such a change. Recent indications of shadow ministers' support for 'higher benefits for higher contributions' suggest that some questions of priorities still need thinking through.

But the overriding characteristics of *Opportunity Britain* are perhaps its caution and conservatism. The extent of redistribution it proposes, at least initially, is limited; and the glosses put on it by shadow ministers suggest that nothing more radical will emerge this side of a general election. There have been pledges that neither corporation tax nor capital gains tax will be increased under a Labour government;[36] the commitment to reintroducing a lower rate band of tax for the low-paid is retreating in time in the same way as the Conservatives' pledge of a 20 pence basic income tax rate; and the abolition of the upper earnings limit on national insurance contributions will be taken into account in setting a higher-rate tax threshold. Whether or not Thatcherism has succeeded in reducing the public's expectations of redistribution by government action, it seems to have succeeded in reducing Labour's. Together with the questioning of the minimum wage policy by union leaders anxious to preserve their members' differentials,[37] these indications mean that anything more than a welcome but modest version of a 'beyond Beveridge' programme from Labour seems unlikely.

Liberal Democrats: citizens' income

The Liberal Democrats perhaps demonstrate the most radical changes to their policy perspective since the last election. The influence of the Social Democratic Party (SDP) led to a confused programme in 1987, in which somehow the means-testing emphasis of the SDP was to slip imperceptibly into the universalist bias of the Liberals. The resulting tax and social security policy was one of the more awkward examples of cooperation in the Alliance.

Now, however, the Liberal Democrats have reverted to the Liberals' traditional affection for tax credits, which would be non-means-tested and would be a means of integrating benefits and tax allowances within one system. This has now been converted to a 'citizens' income', which is a basic income payable to individuals on the basis of residence conditions but not work tests, means tests, contribution tests or marital status.[38] The Liberal Democrats, like most basic income proponents these days, accept that a basic income at subsistence level or above is not possible in the short or medium term. The citizens' income itself would therefore initially only be about £12 per week, and so would need topping up with a low income benefit (income-related but with no capital cut-off) which would replace income support and family credit. Unemployment benefit *was* to be abolished; but, perhaps because of comments from CPAG, the Party has recognised that there may be a case for retaining at least a short-term non-means-tested benefit for unemployment on top of the citizens' income.

The Liberal Democrats' proposals are a technocrat's dream, with pages of detailed figures and complex explanations for further minor adjustments to the framework of benefits. Various analyses and costings of such proposals have been carried out and it is clear that schemes such as this one to introduce a 'partial basic income' can be progressive in their distributional impact. The major problem is political, in that it seems highly unlikely that in the near future it will be acceptable to many people that incomes are delivered to those able to work but not willing to do so – or, at least, not without any test of need. In fact, political thought, not least on the Left, seems to be going further in the direction of emphasising responsibilities rather than unconditional rights, and Ralf Dahrendorf – who provides some of the ideological inspiration for basic income schemes – sometimes seems to be out on a lonesome limb. If this political opposition limited the amount of the proposed partial basic income still further, would the upheaval be worth it for claimants?[39]

Nonetheless, the radical nature of the Liberal Democrats' reforms to tax and social security does challenge all of us to answer fundamental questions about the limits of universality, the implications of real financial independence for women and in particular the suitability of a social security system still based primarily on replacing full-time wages to an increasingly part-time, self-employed and otherwise 'atypical' workforce.

Conclusion

The enterprise culture has become the opportunity society. Fairness appears to have returned as a yardstick for judging public policies. Do we believe this? Are we on the way to a kinder, gentler Britain in the 1990s?

Perhaps. But questions had already been raised about whether there would be sufficient resources to put into practice some of the Thatcher governments' more progressive reforms – for example, the Children Act 1989 and the community care policy due to be implemented in 1993. And there is also the issue of how 'fairness' and 'opportunity' are interpreted, and what kind of a society any 'have-nots' who are provided with opportunities would be entering. The areas of policy examined in this chapter are *not* peripheral, but central to the kind of society the UK is going to be as it approaches the millenium.

First and foremost, it *should* be a society which unambiguously reclaims the economic agenda for social purposes, instead of allowing it to work against them as it did in the 1980s. The market economy cannot, on the evidence of the Thatcher goverments, be regarded as inherently social, as the Chancellor appears to believe.[40] Neither can the most important social priorities once again wait on economic growth, as Labour is warning. A recent study of Britain in 2010 demonstrated that moves towards a more equitable distribution of resources would not necessarily threaten the success of the economy.[41]

How to persuade politicians to tackle poverty at its roots is perhaps something we need to learn from other political movements. The environmentalists, for example, are asking awkward questions such as: growth for what? At whose expense? Anti-poverty strategists involved in the Third World know how crucial economic and property (especially land) reforms are to any social development programme. They also look constantly for ways to enable the poorest people to have more control over their own lives, so that they can help themselves out of their poverty – often in concert with others. And, perhaps most importantly, more of us have learned from them the importance of poverty *prevention*, rather than merely famine relief after the event. It is time that we did the equivalent in the UK in the 1990s. The next chapter examines how this might be done.

Notes

1. Social Security Committee, *Low Income Statistics: Households Below Average Income Tables 1988*, HMSO, 1991. CPAG looks at two possible definitions of poverty derived from official statistics in *Poverty: The Facts* (CPAG Ltd, 1990). This is one of them. (The other is: living at or below supplementary benefit/income support level.)

2. *The Times* (leader), 17 April 1991.

3. See, for example, M Jacques, *The Times*, 12 June 1991.

4. *Independent on Sunday*, 28 April 1991.

5. David Hunt, Secretary of State for Wales, speech on 6 July 1991; Michael Forsyth, Scottish Office Minister, paper for Adam Smith Institute (*Daily Telegraph*, 20 July 1991).

6. For example, the Department of the Environment's press release announcing a survey into the impact of water metering cited CPAG's concerns, as well as the National Consumer Council's.

7. On taking office, on 28 November 1990; and addressing the Conservative Women's Conference on 27 June 1991.

8. Rt Hon John Major MP, 28 November 1990.

9. *Hansard*, 29 November 1990, col 1101.

10. *Daily Telegraph*, 15 April 1991.

11. Rt Hon John Major MP, 28 November 1990; 4 December 1990; 10 February 1991.

12. *Hansard,* 16 May 1991, col 413.

13. J Bradshaw, *Child Poverty and Deprivation in the UK,* National Children's Bureau, 1990; and D Piachaud, 'Revitalising social policy', in *The Political Quarterly,* Vol 62, No 2, 1991, p221.

14. '... we see no permanent place for wages councils in our system' (Michael Howard MP, Secretary of State for Employment (interview in *Financial Times,* 13 May 1991).

15. W W Daniel, *The Unemployed Flow,* Policy Studies Institute, 1990.

16. Rt Hon John Major MP, speaking at the Conservative Women's Conference on 27 June 1991, talked about 'Conservatism' as 'developing personal independence. It is designed to give people a hand-up, not a hand-out...'

17. Rt Hon John Major MP, speech, 23 March 1991.

18. *The Independent,* 6 February 1991.

19. *See* note 17.

20. See R Lister, *The Exclusive Society: Citizenship and the Poor,* CPAG Ltd, 1990.

21. *The Citizen's Charter: Raising the Standard*, HMSO, Cmnd 1599, July 1991; presented in Parliament as a White Paper on 22 July.

22. *See* note 17.

23. *The Independent,* 26 June 1991.

24. See, for example, the leader in the *Financial Times,* 14 May 1991; and Joe Rogaly's article in the *Financial Times,* 26 March 1991. The *Daily Telegraph,* on 10 May 1991, reported that John Major's minute to Ministers asking for ideas on the Citizen's Charter had said that there should be no further strain on the Treasury as a result.

25. Paper given at the 1989 Social Policy Association conference, since published as: R Lister, 'Social security in the 1980s', *Social Policy and Administration*, Vol 25, No 2, 1991.
26. *See* note 17.
27. See *A New Tax for Local Government: A Consultation Paper*, Department of the Environment/Scottish Office/Welsh Office, April 1991.
28. *The Reform of Personal Taxation*, HMSO, 1986.
29. *Financial Times*, 10 May 1991.
30. *The Times*, 8 May 1991.
31. D Lipsey, *The Times*, 28 May 1991, quoting 'a senior Labour figure'.
32. Labour Party, *Opportunity Britain: Labour's Better Way into the 1990s*, April 1991.
33. See, for example, interview with Margaret Beckett MP, Shadow Chief Secretary to the Treasury, in *Poverty*, No 78, CPAG Ltd, Spring 1991.
34. *The Observer*, 29 January 1989.
35. See DHSS, *Reform of Social Security: Programme for Change*, Cmnd 9518, HMSO, 1985, Vol 2, para 4.37.
36. *Financial Times*, 8 May 1991.
37. See, for example, *Daily Telegraph*, 17 June 1991.
38. Social and Liberal Democrats, *Common Benefit: Federal Green Paper*, No 11, December 1989.
39. R Lister, *There is an Alternative: Reforming Social Security*, CPAG Ltd, 1987.
40. Rt Hon Norman Lamont MP, in a speech to the Adam Smith Institute on 12 April 1991, said that his definition of a social market economy was that the framework of law which already exists 'ensures that the social market is an inherently fair way of allocating resources between citizens'.
41. J Northcott, *Britain in 2010*, Policy Studies Institute, 1991.

9.

Conclusions: a new agenda

Saul Becker and Fran Bennett

THIS chapter draws together some of the main themes and issues of the book and identifies the principles and policies needed to promote opportunity and the rights of social citizenship for all – a new agenda for the 1990s.

The Thatcher years

A lost opportunity for the poor

Previous chapters have shown how, for many poor people, the 1980s was a decade of lost opportunities. Almost month by month, one new policy initiative or another worked against the interests, security and stability of people on low incomes (see Appendix for a synopsis of the main events). As part of this strategy, and in the name of wealth creation, Thatcherism always accepted, indeed promoted, inequality (see especially Chapter 2).

In *The Growing Divide*, Ruth Lister put CPAG's alternative view: 'Policies devoted to the creation of greater social cohesion and solidarity would provide a firmer basis for economic growth than our currently divided society.'[1] And as David Donnison has argued: 'A good welfare state, far from being a burden on the productive economy, provides the essential political basis for sound economic policies.'[2]

But the Thatcher government of 1987 again rejected the opportunity to pursue policies necessary to achieve social cohesion and an 'opportunity society' for all. And, as this book has shown, many people in poverty bore the cost not only of the increase in poverty generally, but also of the growth in inequality which took place during the decade as a whole.

Nor were the Thatcher governments' strategies of 'targeting' and 'selectivity' as effective as had been hoped by policy-makers. The intention, as presented during the Fowler review, was that help should be withdrawn from those who did not need it, to be concentrated on those in most need. But this was a very narrow definition of targeting (framed largely in terms of means-testing), which never envisaged a wider redistribution from the better-off to the poor and which did not consider the tax system at all. In the case of the discretionary social fund, perhaps the most extreme example, the targeting was to be done within the boundaries of a pre-defined budget. By becoming supply-led, the social fund effectively replaced the language of 'need' with that of priorities, that is to say, the 'greater need'.[3] The withdrawal of help, during the Thatcher years, from many people deemed not to need it as much as others, did not always result in its concentration on those in greatest need. Convincing evidence that the poorest were, indeed, 'targeted' is not available.

At the same time, it is clear that tax changes greatly helped the better-off, often at the expense of people on low incomes. This inverse redistribution has so often been justified by the certainty of 'trickle-down', but there is no evidence of this effect either.[4] Consequently, poor people lost out on a number of fronts. The cost of this, in terms of blighted opportunities, particularly for women and children in poverty, often remained hidden from public view.

Blaming the victim

Not only were many poor people the victims of Thatcherism's particular cocktail of economic and social policy, but government also seemed to feel that poor people were in some way to blame for their own poverty – a view given ammunition by 'dependency culture' theories imported from the United States. Wider social values, however, appear to have remained relatively stable over the period, despite some of the ambivalence outlined in Chapter 4. The level of support for state welfare remained high throughout the decade, despite Thatcherism's attempts to change the 'hearts and minds' of the public.[5]

Whoever becomes prime minister over the coming year will therefore have a new opportunity, based on a degree of popular support, to establish a new relationship between economic and social policy – a relationship that should promote the rights of social citizenship and opportunities for all.

Working for opportunities

To pursue policies designed to promote an 'opportunity society' for everyone will first require a redefinition of the boundaries between self-reliance and collective responsibility for welfare; between self-interest and collective obligation; and between individual responsibility and rights of entitlement. There should be two inter-related aims of public policy:

- to create *real* opportunities for everyone to participate in society as full citizens; *and*
- to provide freedom from poverty – prevention, rather than simply 'poor relief'.

Opportunity Europe

Consideration of issues of opportunities in Britain can no longer be divorced from the wider issues of citizenship and opportunity in Europe, particularly as we move towards 1992. There is a specific group, or rather mix of groups, which is especially vulnerable to poverty, namely black people. Chapter 7 demonstrates how the issue of race combines with the current legal definition of citizenship to exclude many black people from entitlements granted to their white counterparts, including immigrants from the European Community.

Paul Gordon also points to the dangers of a European mentality which excludes 'outsiders'. A 'Single Market' could become a 'Fortress Europe', hermetically sealed against the outside world. Such a mentality could be counter-productive for those who promote it, since an economically aggressive Europe could provoke precisely the kind of population movements from less strong economies – particularly in the Third World – which it seeks to resist by immigration control. In such a scenario, immigrants – particularly those from non-European countries – and black people will be especially vulnerable to further restrictions of their social rights and opportunities.

Yet the EC dimension could also bring gains to poor people in the UK. The kind of comparisons which Chapter 5 makes have a powerful moral impact when the UK, or indeed any other country, is found wanting compared to other member states. During the first half of the 1980s the UK contributed disproportionately to the increase of poverty in the EC. That this should be exposed by virtue of our membership of the EC is wholly desirable. If 1992 is to mean competition between member states, let them compete in their attempts to eradicate poverty.

And it is not only at the level of comparative propaganda that poor people may stand to gain. In its manifesto for the European Elections in 1989,[6] CPAG pointed to the EC's more positive record in the field of women's rights; and the Social Charter contains a welcome reaffirmation of the Commission's commitment to equal treatment. The Directive on equal treatment of women and men in social security (1978), for example, has proved to be a vital tool in removing sex discrimination in the UK. The Group's manifesto further called for a two-pronged consolidation of that progress – by the implementation of the parental and family leave directive (which gives a right to parents to take leave from their jobs to look after children in specific circumstances), to which the UK government was the only member state to object; and in a directive outlawing discrimination, in social security, against people from ethnic minorities.

Opportunity and citizenship

CPAG believes that public policies which aim to prevent poverty are also those which are most likely to provide real opportunities for all: poverty is the experience of exclusion and powerlessness, as well as lack of money. The denial of opportunity – to participate, to fulfil personal potential, to move forward, to have hope – is a particularly destructive part of that experience.

Policies to promote opportunity need to be placed within a wider strategy, which works towards effective social citizenship for all. In *The Exclusive Society*, Ruth Lister outlined a Charter for Social Citizenship. She argued that 'a society which excludes many of its members from full citizenship puts itself at risk… We must put an end to the divisive policies of exclusion and start rebuilding the solid foundations that an effective web of citizenship rights can provide.'[7] The quests for real rights of social citizenship and for 'windows of opportunity' go hand-in-hand. Public policies on taxation and social security, on employment and training, on public services and caring, should aim to ensure that 'all members of society have sufficient income to enable them to meet their public and private obligations as citizens and to exercise effectively their legal, political and social rights as citizens'.[8]

New directions

CPAG has set out elsewhere the general principles which flow from its thinking about how the prevention of poverty would be achieved in practice.[9] Here we examine some of the directions in which such principles would take us, and some of the issues which would confront any political party today which attempted to move in those directions. As previous chapters have demonstrated, we live in a changing world. Employment patterns are shifting, with more temporary and part-time jobs and self-employment on the increase. Family structures are altering, and there are more lone-parent families and very elderly people. The UK is increasingly a multi-racial and multi-cultural society and is becoming more and more influenced by its European neighbours. More women are looking for greater financial independence. As we adapt to these changes, we need to rethink how to put our values and our principles into practice – and, crucially, how to avoid the creation of new insecurities and new inequalities.

Any broad strategy to tackle the *causes* of poverty and social division cannot focus on the social security system alone (although we look at this central area of CPAG's work in more detail). We have to look at the full range of policies which affect all of us in the UK. We have to find ways of preventing poverty, rather than just picking up the pieces.

The distribution and quality of employment opportunities are crucially important. The taxation system is an instrument not merely to raise money but also to affect the allocation of resources between different income groups. And access to high quality services is an important contributor to standards of living, especially for families on low incomes. We look at each of these areas in turn below.

Employment opportunities

As Chapter 8 emphasises, a reduction in unemployment is central to creating opportunities for children, whose life chances are blighted and blocked by their parents' unemployment. The assumption that governments have no responsibility for the level of unemployment must be challenged. And special measures are needed to redress the disadvantages in access to employment and training for certain groups, including women, black people, people with disabilities and the long-term unemployed. This notion, previously accepted in principle by governments of both major parties, needs now to be taken further.

The trend of current policies inexorably tends towards a belief in 'a job at any price'. But jobs without employment protection and security, subsidised by means-tested benefits (where these are taken up), and vulnerable to damaging changes in contracts and even redundancy, cannot provide the basis to build personal security. And on the strength of US experience, 'workfare' does not provide a long-term means of integrating marginal workers into the core labour force.[10] Many of our European neighbours have much stronger statutory minimum wage provision, employment protection and employment rights than does the UK. Their experience does not support the view that this impedes economic performance.

CPAG has long supported a statutory national minimum wage. It is not the Group's role to comment extensively on econometric models about the likely employment effects. But, leaving aside the international comparisons, it must be observed that, if the introduction of a minimum wage at an adequate level is believed to cause unemployment in specific sectors, the answer cannot be the indiscriminate subsidy provided to all employers paying low wages to certain categories of employees which family credit currently represents, and which the disability working allowance will in future extend. Indeed, the profile of family credit claimants, which shows that the vast majority are either lone parents or two-parent, one-earner families, would suggest that a strategy to reduce reliance on means-tested benefits by wage-earners would need to encompass, in addition to a minimum wage, improved equal pay legislation on the one hand and increased provision of childcare on the other.

Taxation

The programme set out here would both necessitate and result in shifts in public expenditure and taxation, reversing the trends of the last thirteen years. To pay for the benefits which we want to see, it will be necessary to reduce the 'alternative welfare state' currently provided through the array of income tax reliefs and exemptions which, in their extent, approach the size of the social security budget. These undermine the position of the poor in relative terms by benefiting the better-off most, and in absolute terms by eroding the tax base necessary for benefits and other provision to be financed.

The question of 'fairness' in taxation was unavoidably raised in the public debate about the poll tax – not least by CPAG.[11] It is back on the agenda. And the moves in the 1991 Budget (see Chapter 8) to limit the additional tax advantages enjoyed by married couples and by mortgage-payers on higher-rate tax have carried the principle another step forward. But neither of the two main parties appears to be challenging sufficiently the 'double standard' employed by the Treasury, which treats public expenditure as 'bad' and foregone revenue through tax reliefs and allowances as 'good'.

CPAG believes that the tax system as a whole should be made more progressive,[12] in particular through the reintroduction of a series of stepped income tax rates above the basic rate. The national insurance contribution scheme is still a major factor in the regressiveness of parts of the overall tax system – despite some welcome reforms in recent years for both employees and employers. The upper earnings limit should be abolished for employees. CPAG would like to see all tax reliefs and allowances allowed against the basic rate of tax only, pending an examination of the rationale for each of them. The recent inquiry into housing, chaired by the Duke of Edinburgh, has again put the total (phased) abolition of mortgage interest tax relief on the agenda, providing the resources for a more rational system of housing finance.[13] Although none of the major parties is likely to commit itself to this move before the election, we must hope that the growing support for it will bear fruit during the decade.

The case for an individually-based tax system has, again, been accepted in part with the recent introduction of so-called 'independent taxation'. But it is marred by the continuation of the married couple's allowance (still paid in the first instance to the husband, unless he cannot take advantage of it). The freezing of the married couple's allowance should be continued, with a government pledge to spend the resulting resources on cash benefits going direct to children and carers. This is a major opportunity for the community as a whole to share more in the costs of caring for the *true* dependants in society.

The taxation of capital and wealth should be made more effective, reversing the changes of recent years. (This is particularly important in view of the increasing significance of the inheritance of owner-occupied housing at the most prosperous stage of the lifecycle.)[14] All the major parties are now committed to exempting the poorest from local tax altogether, which CPAG welcomes; but the structure of local taxation should still be made more progressive overall, with a reform of the grant allocation system to equalise resources between worse-off and better-off areas. The increases in direct and indirect taxation over the last decade have disadvantaged those on low incomes; CPAG supports the government's continued resistance to any erosion of zero-rating for younger children's clothing and shoes.

Quality services

Anti-poverty measures cannot be confined to income alone; adequate public services are increasingly recognised as a vital contribution to overall standards of living and quality of life. While we do not accept the conflation of citizenship and consumerism of the Citizen's Charter,[15] if it is successful in its objectives it could be of real advantage to poor people who depend more on public services and who tend to get a worse deal from them. However, without the backing of extra resources any improvements are likely to be limited.

A Charter which genuinely addressed the role public services could play in promoting citizenship and opportunity, for children in particular, would recognise the need for a reversal of the current trend towards educational opportunities being increasingly determined by parental income through contributions to essential school equipment and facilities. It would guarantee an end to the situation in which so many children's lives, and health, are damaged by homelessness, or by having to exist in bed and breakfast accommodation or the under-resourced public housing sector. It would increase quality childcare provision, which is crucial not just as a determinant of employment oportunities for women, but also to expand children's experiences. The need for employers to attract more women into the workforce should add to the pressure for increased provision, but should not be allowed on its own to determine the form of that provision – the needs of children should come first. CPAG believes that more public finance for childcare provision provides a better way forward than introducing yet another specific tax relief, which would benefit the higher-paid most.

Putting 'security' back into social security

The principles and policies identified above are essential to a coherent strategy to promote real opportunities and a fairer future for children and for all. Social security provision cannot be expected to compensate adequately for many difficulties whose root causes lie elsewhere. Economic and employment-related policies are a major determinant of poverty and social divisions; they should therefore be a major focus of action to tackle them. But benefit provision is nonetheless central, both to an anti-poverty strategy and to CPAG's own work. Listed here are some broad goals, therefore, for an improved social security system. We need:

- **Benefits which are high enough to ensure that no one is excluded from full participation in the life of society simply because they lack money.** A full assessment, by government, of what exactly should be provided for by benefits – and their adequacy for different claimant groups – will therefore be necessary. The work currently being done by both the Family Budget Unit[16] and the Social Security Select Committee should be a useful contribution to this task. CPAG believes that the most urgent priority needs are those of families with children and long-term unemployed people – both groups which are consistently shown to be under the greatest pressure when living on benefit. And benefit claimants cannot be allowed to fall increasingly far behind the rest of the population, in the way they do when benefits are uprated in line with prices only.

- **Benefits which move away from discretion and towards rights of entitlement.** The government has been put on the defensive recently over the discretionary provisions for both 16- and 17-year-olds and students who have lost automatic entitlement to benefit. But the unfairness and administrative costs of these discretionary provisions are outweighed in volume by those of the social fund, to which both the National Audit Office and the Public Accounts Committee have drawn attention.[17] Ministers are still defending the social fund against all criticism,[18] but much constructive work has been done, by CPAG and others, to devise an alternative and better scheme for one-off regular and emergency needs,[19] which needs to be built upon in the run-up to the election.

- **Benefits which move away from means-testing and towards entitlement based on category of claimant or 'contingency'.** Criticisms of the growing dependence on means-tested benefits has been voiced increasingly by commentators usually associated with right-wing thought,[20] as well as by more traditional critics. We need to build on this development. Reliance on means tests and contribution tests to determine eligibility should, as far as possible, be phased out or reduced.

- **Benefits which allow individual adults to live as autonomously as possible.** If means-tested benefits are relied upon less, personal autonomy will be strengthened as it becomes more feasible for the individual to be the unit of assessment. Means-testing is likely always to involve a joint assessment of income and other resources – just one of its many disadvantages. (But when means-tested benefits are awarded on this basis, payment could nonetheless be made direct to individuals – as is done already with community charge benefit.)[21] Individually-based benefit rights are particularly important in a situation of increasing instability of family units.

- **Benefits which are delivered in a way which ensures equal access to, and equal treatment from, the social security system for all claimants.** The Benefits Agency, created in April 1991, has ambitions to make the system more 'user-friendly', but is finding it impossible to achieve them without sufficient resources.[22] More user involvement in the delivery of benefits – as happens in some other countries – would ensure that the system really answered to claimants' requirements. The recent report by the National Association of Citizens' Advice Bureaux[23] demonstrated how far there is to go before black and ethnic minority claimants are treated equally by the benefits system.

- **Benefits which fulfil two central functions adequately: to meet additional costs and to provide income replacement.** The additional costs to be met by benefits include in particular those for children and those to meet the extra costs of people with disabilities. The value CPAG puts on child benefit is well-known, and its advantages are summarised below. We are delighted that all three main parties are now committed to retaining child benefit. But the government's new structure for the benefit, with its bonus for the eldest child, has yet to be adequately justified (other than politically, as a cheap means of giving an increase in child benefit to every family). And there is still a long way to go before CPAG's long-term goal for child benefit to meet the minimum costs of a child is realised, thus removing the need for additional benefits for most children within the social security system. In particular, the significant amounts paid in family credit could not be matched unless a multi-pronged strategy is adopted (see above).

The new disability living allowance, merging mobility and attendance allowance but also introducing a lower rate, has been rightly criticised by disability organisations for ignoring the many other costs of disability. But the new self-assessment and adjudication procedures may mean that there is now a better basis on which to build a comprehensive disability income to meet wider additional costs.

Benefits to provide an income replacement for those unable to support themselves through paid employment obviously cover a much wider area, which it is not possible to discuss in detail here. CPAG's priorities would be to extend unemployment benefit to long-term unemployed people and to pay it at a higher rate (as other long-term benefits are), as well as to reverse the recent restrictions on entitlement which have affected women in particular. As Ruth Lister noted in *There is an Alternative*,[24] many problems need to be thought through in developing such a benefits system, including its relationship with occupational benefits (still growing in significance), and the vexed question of how to improve the incomes of claimants on means-tested benefits while simultaneously lifting as many people as possible out of their scope. Any non-contributory system would also move away from earnings-relation which, although it has been virtually removed by the present government, is widely used by our European partners. There may be a limit to how much social security by itself can modify the inequalities of rewards in the labour market. But any earnings-related system will inevitably reflect the disadvantaged position of those disabled from birth, as well as those with interrupted and/or 'marginal' work records.

A new opportunity: a new agenda

Central to CPAG's concerns is the shape of the future for families with children, especially those on low incomes. This must also be a central concern for society as a whole, since children represent *our* future. The latest statistics from the social fund show that for 1990-91, one in four of our children were born into families on means-tested benefits.[25] We cannot, and must not, countenance a situation in which a quarter of our children thus begin their lives in the poverty and insecurity which means-tested benefits bring.

To tackle this situation will require attention to meeting more adequately both the direct and indirect costs of children. CPAG has focused more on the former, and in particular on the potential of child benefit. Uniquely it helps families at the most vulnerable stage of their lifecycle, and helps one- and two-parent families and one- and two-earner families alike.[26] More resources being put into child benefit would thus help to resolve some of the more difficult issues of family policy currently under discussion. And all this for the minimum of administrative costs. Child benefit remains a cornerstone of CPAG's policy.

But we must also pay more attention to the *indirect* costs of children, which currently fall largely on families themselves and particularly on women within those families. How to combine the recent expansion of 'second earners'' employment with ways to make such employment more secure and better rewarded is a fundamental challenge facing us in the 1990s. And the experiences of our European partners would suggest that we should go further in the provision of public finance for childcare, in particular for 3- to 5-year-olds, and after-school and holiday provision for school-aged children.

The mixed messages of public opinion polls described in Chapter 4 show how far there is still to go before wider social attitudes truly reflect the realities of poverty and social exclusion. But they also demonstrate the potential for turning concern into commitment to change, towards a society in which a fairer future and real opportunities for all become a top priority.

So this book concludes with a call to politicians of all major parties, and to the public as a whole, to develop a comprehensive strategy to bring about freedom from poverty, and freedom from the fear of poverty, for all families. As we move forward to the twenty-first century, we have to think of leaving poverty behind, rather than leaving poor people behind.

Notes

1. R Lister, 'Conclusion II: There is an alternative', in A Walker and C Walker (eds), *The Growing Divide: A Social Audit 1979-87* , CPAG Ltd, 1987, pp148-49.
2. *The Observer*, 9 June 1985.
3. S Becker and R Silburn, *The New Poor Clients*, Community Care/Benefits Research Unit, 1990, pp78-79.
4. J Bradshaw, *Child Poverty and Deprivation in the UK*, National Children's Bureau, 1990.
5. See, for example, J Rentoul, 'Individualism', in R Jowell, S Witherspoon and L Brook (eds), *British Social Attitudes: The 7th Report*, Gower, 1990; and P Taylor-Gooby, 'Social welfare: the unkindest cuts' in the same volume, p2.
6. CPAG, *Europe: a fairer future*, CPAG Ltd, 1989.
7. R Lister, *The Exclusive Society: Citizenship and the Poor*, CPAG Ltd, 1990, p73.
8. *See* note 7, p71.
9. See, for example, R Lister, *There is an Alternative: Reforming Social Security*, CPAG Ltd, 1987; and R Lister, *see* note 1.
10. R Walker, *Thinking about Workfare: Evidence from the USA*, SPRU/HMSO, 1991.
11. See, for example, C Oppenheim, *A Tax on all the People: The Poll Tax*, CPAG Ltd, 1987; and P Esam and C Oppenheim, *A Charge on the Community: The Poll Tax, Benefits and the Poor*, CPAG Ltd/LGIU, 1989.
12. John Hills set out some ideas for such reforms in *Changing Tax: How the Tax System Works and How to Change It*, CPAG Ltd, 1988.
13. *Inquiry into British Housing: Second Report, June 1991*, Joseph Rowntree Foundation, June 1991.
14. See, for example, P Ormerod and M Willmott, 'Willpower – home ownership, inheritance and the next century', in *Poverty* No 73, CPAG Ltd, Summer 1989.
15. *The Citizen's Charter: Raising the Standard*, HMSO, Cmnd 1599, July 1991; presented in Parliament as a White Paper on 22 July.
16. See, for example, J Bradshaw and J Ernst, *Establishing a Modest but Adequate Budget for a British Family*, Working Paper no 2, Family Budget Unit/ Joseph Rowntree Foundation, June 1990.
17. National Audit Office, *The Social Fund*, House of Commons Paper 190, HMSO, February 1991; Committee of Public Accounts, *The Social Fund*, 24th Report, Session 1990/91, HMSO, May 1991.
18. See, for example, the article by Nicholas Scott MP, Minister for Social Security and Disabled People, in *Social Work Today*, 23 May 1991.
19. Some examples are set out by Gary Craig in *Poverty* No 77, Winter 1990/91,

and by Richard Berthoud in *Poverty* No 79, Summer 1991, CPAG Ltd.

20. See, for example, J C Brown, *Child Benefit: Options for the 1990s*, Save Child Benefit, July 1990, in which she quotes Lord (Keith) Joseph and the National Family Trust, amongst others.

21. For a discussion of these issues, see J Roll, *What is a Family? Benefit Models and Social Realities,* Family Policy Studies Centre, June 1991.

22. Michael Bichard, chief executive of the Benefits Agency, quoted in *The Independent*, 26 June 1991.

23. *Barriers to Benefit: Black Claimants and Social Security,* National Association of Citizens' Advice Bureaux, January 1991.

24. *See* note 9.

25. Calculated by Maternity Alliance with reference to Annex 1, *Annual Report by the Secretary of State for Social Security on the Social Fund 1990/91*, HMSO, Cmnd 1580, July 1991.

26. *See* note 20.

Appendix

The Conservatives' diary

Policies affecting poor families: June 1979 - July 1991

Jill Vincent

1979

June: Budget: income tax cuts benefit highest paid most; tax cuts outweighed by increase in VAT for those on average earnings or below; prescription charges rise from 20p to 45p and some dental charges rise; 50p increase in one parent benefit but no increase in child benefit.

September: Social Security (Claims and Payments) Amendment Regulations: unemployment benefit henceforth to be paid fortnightly, except for those on short-time working or who choose to be paid weekly.

November: Previous year's shortfall in uprating of short-term benefits not made good. Pensions and other long-term benefits not fully protected against increase in VAT.

1980

February: Price of school meals raised from 30p to 35p. 1,050 extra DHSS staff employed on anti-fraud work.

March: Budget: child benefit to be increased by 75p in November (but £1.20 increase required to restore April 1979 value); instead, improvements made in one parent benefit and family income supplement; lower rate band of tax abolished.

April: Prescription charges rise to 70p and charges for dental treatment up; charge of £2 for a sight test (except for under-16s). Council house rents up on average by 21 per cent. National insurance contributions up by 0.25 per cent.

July: Social Security Act 1980: provides for breaking of link between earnings and benefits uprating and for changes to supplementary benefit system. Social Security (No 2) Act 1980: provides for abolition of earnings-related supplement, 5 per cent abatement of short-term national insurance benefits and invalidity benefit and cuts in strikers' and various other benefits (*see* November 1980 and January 1982). Education (No. 2) Act: local education authorities (LEAs) no longer required to provide nursery education, school meals (other than for children in families in receipt of supplementary benefit or family income supplement); LEAs can now charge and provide what they wish.

November: Social Security Act 1980: Supplementary Benefit Commission abolished and some functions replaced by Social Security Advisory Committee. New supplementary benefit scheme comes into effect (*see* July 1980). National insurance and supplementary benefit rates aligned, thus reducing supplementary pensions by 40p pw. Claimants lose two weeks of increase due to November uprating taking effect two weeks later than normal. Pensions and other long-term benefit increases linked to estimates of price rises only; consequently lower than if still related to earnings. Short-term and invalidity benefits increased by 5 per cent less than forecast of estimate of price rises (*see* July 1980). Changes made in method of uprating national insurance child dependency additions, resulting in cuts in real value of child support in this and subsequent years. Family income supplement and mobility allowance raised by more than inflation.

December: Prescription charges up to £1. School-leavers denied supplementary benefit until end of school holidays after they leave.

1981

March: Budget: personal tax allowances frozen but child benefit increased in line with inflation. Social Security Act 1981: intention to claw back in November 1 per cent overpaid in 1980 because of overestimate of inflation.

April: Social Security Contributions Act 1981: provides for increase in range of low earnings over which national insurance contributions paid and for a reduction in Treasury supplement to national insurance fund, thus requiring an increase in contribution rates higher than that required by Government Actuary. Council house rents up on average by 45 per cent. National insurance contributions up by 1 per cent.

July: Extension of long-term rate of supplementary benefit for men 60 or over

if unemployed for one year or more and cease registering for work. Patrick Jenkin commits government to maintain child benefit at November 1980 value, subject to economic and other circumstances. Poverty figures to be published biennially rather than annually.

September: Education Act 1980: assisted places scheme comes into effect; free school meals for assisted pupils in families in receipt of supplementary benefit or family income supplement; half-price meals for assisted pupils not eligible for free meals but whose parents' income up to £4,000 pa. Initial uniform grants up to £80 and subsequent grants of £20-£40 every second year; free travel for pupils living more than 3 miles from school if parental income up to £4,600, and a sliding scale determining charges for those with higher incomes.

November: 1 per cent clawback on benefit increases; shortfall in benefit uprating – 2 per cent lower than inflation, except mobility allowance raised by more than rate of inflation.

December: Chancellor announces he will restore the shortfall only to certain long-term beneficiaries.

1982

January: Social Security (No 2) Act 1980: earnings-related supplement to unemployment, sickness, widows' and maternity benefits start to be phased out.

March: Budget: 2 per cent shortfall to be restored for all benefits; child benefit to be increased in line with inflation; personal tax allowances to be raised by more than inflation; no statement on restoration of 5 per cent abatement on unemployment benefit when brought into tax (*see* July 1982); mobility allowance to be tax-free. New mothers to receive child benefit monthly; existing recipients and a limited group of new recipients can opt to continue to receive a weekly payment (eg, lone parents).

April: Prescription charges rise to £1.30; glasses up from £8.30 to £15 per lens; charges for routine dental treatment from £9 maximum to £13 maximum. Council house rents up on average by 19 per cent. National insurance contributions up by 1 per cent.

June: Government announces lone mothers claiming one parent benefit not to be asked about their sex lives. Self-certification of sickness introduced.

July: Unemployment benefit becomes taxable; attempts by Conservative backbenchers to restore 5 per cent abatement fail. Expectant mothers no longer required to satisfy national insurance contribution conditions to receive maternity grant (though have to satisfy 26-week residence rule).

October: End of compulsory registration at job centres and consequent changes in method of counting unemployed people and in 'availability for work' test.

November: Social Security and Housing Benefits Act 1982: housing benefit payable to some council tenants in receipt of supplementary benefit (*see* also April 1983). Supplementary benefit uprated on basis of Retail Price Index minus housing element, ie, at 0.5 per cent less than other benefits. Increase in supplementary benefit capital limit to £2,500. Chancellor announces intention to claw back this year's overestimate of rate of inflation.

December: Postal claims introduced for unemployed supplementary benefit claimants.

1983

March: Child benefit increased by 11 per cent – making good previous cut; tax allowances increased by 14 per cent.

April: Industrial injury benefit abolished. Social Security and Housing Benefit Act 1982: statutory sick pay introduced: first eight weeks of sick pay responsibility of employers – low rates for low-paid; no additions for dependants; taxable and subject to national insurance contributions. Prescription charges rise to £1.40. National insurance contributions up by 0.25 per cent. Housing benefit payable instead of rent rebates and allowances for all tenants and instead of rate rebates for tenants, and owner-occupiers (*see* also November 1982).

April: Widespread chaos results from implementation of housing benefit. Thousands of tenants receive either no benefit or wrong amount due to computer or administrative error. SHAC reports 2.5m tenants worse off as a result of scheme. Regulations published allowing married women to claim national insurance dependency additions.

July: Prime Minister refuses to give assurance that unemployment benefit will be increased in line with inflation like other national insurance benefits.

August: Department of Employment steps up drive against alleged fraud with establishment of Regional Benefit Investigation Teams.

October: DHSS Low Income Families Tables show rising tide of poverty in Great Britain.

November: Chancellor's Autumn statement: housing programme cut by £465m in 1984/85, housing benefit by £230m; 5 per cent abatement of unemployment benefit, but not other benefits, made good; statutory sick pay does not compensate for 5 per cent abatement of sickness benefit; benefits uprated on historical method, not prediction of inflation: increase 2 per cent less than under old method. Invalidity trap abolished. Review of pensions announced.

December: Abolition of 'normal household duties test' and replacement of non-contributory invalidity pension and housewives' NCIP by severe disablement allowance announced.

1984

January: Conservative backbench revolt forces government to modify proposed housing benefit cut to £185m.

February: DHSS orders major drive in 59 areas into alleged social security abuse: unemployment review officers question 18-25-year-olds about why they left jobs; Social Security Policy Inspectorate interviews young people not joining a YTS scheme. White Paper outlines huge reduction in spending on school meals from £414m in 1983/84 to £257m in 1984/85; Hertfordshire County Council first local authority to abolish school meals for all children except those statutorily entitled to them. Review of housing benefit announced. Government refuses to lend Britain's support to UN-sponsored International Year for the Homeless.

March: Further increase in prescription charges to £1.60. Budget: tax allowances raised by 12 per cent. Child benefit increases no longer announced as part of Budget.

April: Secretary of State for Social Services announces 'most comprehensive review of social security system for 40 years'. Estimates show 2.5m people worse off following housing benefit cuts.

May: Review of maternity benefits announced.

June: November benefit upratings announced, together with cuts of over £100m; Social Security Minister Rhodes Boyson says almost 2m disabled and elderly people face benefit cuts of 50p to £1. Child benefit increased by less than increase in personal tax allowances.

September: DHSS announces six-month freeze on amounts of supplementary benefit paid to people in board and lodgings and in private or voluntary residential homes.

October: Patrick Jenkin announces departmental enquiry into local government finance, including 'whether local democratic accountability could be improved by reducing rate rebates so that poor people would feel full cost of council spending'. Most married women excluded from Community Programme by new regulation requiring Community Programme people or their spouse to be on unemployment benefit or supplementary benefit.

November: Chancellor's Autumn statement: substantial restrictions on payment of supplementary benefit for those in lodgings and private residential and nursing homes; proposed increase in housing benefit children's needs allowance cancelled; 5 per cent abatement in invalidity pension restored but invalidity pensioners no longer to receive both earnings-related component and age-related invalidity allowance at same time. Public expenditure on housing cut by £65m for 1985/86 although Treasury had planned £650m cut.

1985

January: Social Security Commissioners rule that strikers not entitled to family income supplement on basis of strike income.

February: Social Security Minister announces that postal claiming to be made available to all supplementary benefit claimants by end of May.

March: Budget: real increase in tax

thresholds and restructuring of national insurance contributions announced; new regulations result in housing benefit cuts of up to £5.47pw for 110,000 tenants in high rent areas. DHSS announces regulations forcing unemployed 16-25-year-olds in board and lodgings to move every two, four or eight weeks according to area, or face big cuts in benefit.

April: 25 per cent increase in dental charges: dentists claim that patients not exempt from charges would pay most of cost of their treatment for the first time. Total abolition of 'half-test' rule for married women announced.

May: Government Green Paper proposes means-testing home improvement grants. Her Majesty's Inspectorate of Schools reports expenditure cuts on school buildings adversely affecting quality of education.

June: Green Paper on review of social security published. 35p cut in child benefit announced as part of benefit uprating; 850,000 families with a young unemployed, disabled or pensioner relative living at home to have reduction in housing benefit.

July: Following an earlier consultation paper, Employment Secretary announces intention to introduce early legislation to remove all young people under 21 from wages council regulations and confine councils to setting only a single minimum rate and a single overtime rate for those 21 and over. Proposals to allow employers to opt out of statutory sick pay published in consultative document 'Lifting the Burden'. MSC extends YTS to two years for 500,000 young people. Enquiry into British housing, chaired by Duke of Edinburgh, recommends abolition of mortgage interest tax relief.

August: High Court finds government restrictions on board and lodgings payments unlawful.

September: DHSS appeals against High Court decision on board and lodgings regulations – government again defeated in Court of Appeal.

October: New temporary regulations to curb board and lodging supplementary benefit payments also declared unlawful by House of Commons Statutory Instruments Committee; regulations subsequently withdrawn.

November: Environment Secretary Kenneth Baker announces £185m cut in capital spending on housing; GLC reports 700 per cent rise in official homelessness since 1970.

December: White Paper on Social Security published incorporating certain changes to Green Paper, including proposal that state earnings-related pension scheme not be abolished, but modified.

1986

January: Social Security Bill introduced into Commons. Secretary of State for Scotland announces replacement of domestic rates with poll tax on all adult residents.

February: Housing Minister states that rent controls for new tenants to be phased out after next general election. Cuts in legal aid, particularly hurting low-income families with children, announced.

March: Budget: basic rate of income tax reduced to 29 per cent and personal allowances raised by 5.7 per cent in line with inflation. Green Paper on Reform of Personal Taxation proposes transferable allowances for married couples.

April: European Court finds Britain in breach of EEC law on sex discrimination by refusing to pay invalid care allowance to married and cohabiting women. Statutory sick pay extended from eight to 28 weeks.

May: White Paper 'Building Businesses ... Not Barriers' proposes removing or reducing a number of employees' rights.

June: Comprehensive review of student grants, including possibility of introducing loans, announced. Government announces savings of £100m from cuts in housing benefit.

July: Social Security Act 1986 and Wages Act 1986 receive Royal Assent. DHSS *Low Income Families Tables* released as House of Commons begins summer recess. Restart scheme for long-term unemployed launched, including compulsory interviews – individuals failing to attend interviews or refusing 'available work', risk having benefit suspended for up to 13 weeks (from October).

August: Cuts in supplementary benefit single payments introduced. Revised exceptionally severe weather payments scheme announced for some supplementary benefit claimants. Department of Environment figures show annual number of families accepted as homeless is 94,000.

October: Under 1986 Social Security Act changes in industrial injuries scheme implemented; voluntary unemployment penalty extended from 6 to 13 weeks and reduced rates of short-term national insurance benefits abolished. Announced that benefits to be increased by 2 per cent in April 1987. No restoration of 35p cut in child benefit made in 1985. Expenditure on housing benefit to be reduced by £68m: average loss of 47p per week for pensioners and 56p for other claimants. Tightening up of procedures for assessing availability for work of newly unemployed announced.

November: Chancellor's autumn statement: statutory sick pay to be cut by £18.5m pa, housing programme to be increased by 14 per cent, for repairs to existing properties rather than new building.

1987

January: Government announces trigger temperature for exceptionally severe weather payments to be increased in response to 'severest weather for 40 years'. Supplementary benefit claimants under pension age to receive only half mortgage interest for first 4 months on benefit; further freeze on board and lodging supplementary benefit payments announced.

March: Further increase in prescription charges announced: a 12-fold cash increase of 1,100 per cent since 1979. Budget: basic rate of tax cut by 2p; personal allowances increased in line with inflation; Chancellor widely criticised for failing to help unemployed people and low-paid. Health Education Council's Report, *The Health Divide,* published, showing social inequalities in health widening in the 1980s.

April: Abolition of £25 maternity grant for all mothers: women on family income supplement and supplementary benefit can apply to newly-established social fund; statutory maternity pay paid by employers replaces maternity benefit; abolition of death grant and replacement by help from social fund for those on family income supplement, housing benefit or supplementary benefit .

May: Announcement that income support to include compensation for average amounts claimants are expected to pay towards rates.

June: Mrs Thatcher wins a third term. Queen's speech confirms that 16-17-year-olds who refuse a YTS place will lose their right to benefit and that a community charge (poll tax) will be introduced in England and Wales, a year after it is to be introduced in Scotland (*see* January 1986).

July: Government states that poll tax will be phased in over four years, beginning in April 1990 at a target figure of £100 per adult. From April 1988 everyone liable for rates will contribute at least 20 per cent. Regulations under Social Security Act 1986 published, to come into operation in April 1988.

September: Government publishes plans to revive private sector in rented housing, to widen choice for tenants and restrict role of local government.

October: Participation in Community Programme schemes is limited to people unemployed for 12 months or more. Benefit uprating announcement: child benefit to be frozen, social fund budget to be set at about £200m. Figures for new income support rates for April 1988 reveal cuts of 50p per adult. Plans announced for 300 extra fraud investigators.

November: Announced that from April 1988 government will double to six months period people are disqualified from unemployment benefit if they become voluntarily unemployed, saving £37m in a full year. Minister of Health announces abolition of free dental check-ups and eye tests.

December: Error in past inflation measure detected: some claimants compensated.

1988

February: White Paper signals demise of Community Programme, to be replaced by schemes which pay benefit plus a small top-up. Further measures announced to counter benefit fraud and to tighten up 'availability for work' testing.

March: Budget: reduces top tax rate from 60 per cent to 40 per cent and basic tax rate to 25 per cent; 'independent' taxation to be introduced – married man's tax allowance to be replaced by a married couple's allowance (to man in first instance). Local Government Finance Bill brings in poll tax – Conservative back-

bench MPs reduce government's majority to 25 over a proposed 'ability to pay' system, and to 63 for Bill itself.

April: Prescription charges up by 20p to £2.60. Social Security Act 1986, heralded as most fundamental reform since Beveridge, comes fully into force: income support replaces supplementary benefit, family credit replaces family income supplement, social fund replaces single and urgent needs payments. After controversy, capital limit raised from £6,000 to £8,000 for housing benefit. Employees can choose between occupational pension schemes, SERPS and personal pension schemes. Government calculates that 35 per cent of supplementary benefit claimants will lose, 46 per cent will gain, rest will stay the same. Others calculate far higher proportions of losers. Government announces that poll tax rebates will be extended to over a million more as taper is reduced from 20 per cent (under rate rebates) to 15 per cent under poll tax rebates.

May: Government publishes first edition of new statistical series, *Households Below Average Income* (HBAI), for 1981, 1983 and 1985, with final edition of *Low Income Families* (LIF) for same years. LIF Tables show that in 1985, 9.3 million people were living on or below supplementary benefit level. HBAI Tables show rise in real income after housing costs of 8.4 per cent for bottom tenth of population, in comparison with 4.8 per cent for average (*see* also April 1990); between 1979 and 1985 a 100 per cent increase to 4.02m people in families with children living at or below this 'poverty line', and a 55 per cent increase to 6.45m people in families with children living in poverty or on its margins. National Audit Office report criticises service in local DHSS offices, especially time taken to clear claims and accuracy.

July: DHSS split into Department of

Social Security (DSS) and Department of Health (DH).

September: Employment Training (ET) scheme starts, giving 600,000 people per year average of 6 months' training on 'benefit plus' (*see* February 1988). 16-17-year-olds can no longer claim income support if required to be available for work, except where 'severe hardship'. DES publishes draft guidelines on charges for school activities. Government announces it is to abolish Training Commission (formerly MSC). First in series of OPCS reports on disability published, showing over 6 million disabled adults.

October: New, more restrictive conditions for contributory benefits which cut 40,000 people from unemployment count. SHAC and Shelter say homelessness has doubled in 11 years since Housing (Homeless Persons) Act.

November: Second OPCS disability survey shows disabled adults have to spend extra £6.10 per week on average. New cold weather payments scheme implemented. White Paper proposes that student grants be frozen and replaced with loans from 1990/91; full-time students will no longer be eligible for income support, unemployment benefit or housing benefit (*see* July 1990).

1989

January: Review of NHS sets out key changes, including self-governing status, new funding systems for Health Authorities and own budgets for GPs.

February: Local Government and Housing Bill sets out further measures to remove housing provision from local authorities and to control their housing finance.

March: Budget: changes to national insurance contributions (*see* October). 16-17-year-olds living independently to get higher income support; housing bene-fit increased for all 16-17-year-olds. Payments to young people leaving care to be disregarded for benefit purposes. Government announces establishment of Training and Enterprise Councils to coordinate local training, to be run by business.

April: Child benefit frozen for second year running; average of 50p extra per child added to child rates of income support. Social fund budget frozen for second year. Housing benefit transitional protection reduced by £2 per week. Prescriptions up 20p to £2.80; payment for sight tests introduced. Introduction of poll tax in Scotland. Changes to benefits for board and lodging claimants; and abolition of time limits (*see* March 1985).

May: Plans announced to introduce agency status for majority of social security operations. Secretary of State John Moore's speech, 'The end of the line for poverty', argues that absolute poverty no longer exists, that relative poverty is no more than inequality and that academics and others are really just attacking capitalism.

June: 50-plus Jobstart launched: over 50s to get £20 a week in part-time jobs of ten hours a week or more and paying less than £2.57 an hour.

July: Social fund officers warned they are overspending budgets and will have to cut back.

August: Over 2.85m people were not getting benefit to which they are entitled and nearly £1.2bn in means-tested benefits went unclaimed in 1985/86. Leaked document from DSS shows poll tax debts are to be deducted directly from benefits.

October: Additional premiums for very elderly and disabled people on income support. Institute for Fiscal Studies report that new poverty statistics introduced by government removed 1m people from the poorest group. 'Actively seeking work' replaces 'availability for work' for unemployment benefit claimants, thus imposing stricter eligibility test. Abolition of earnings rule for pensioners. Employees' national insurance contributions 2 per cent of earnings up to lower earnings limit and 9 per cent above.

November: All 16-17-year-olds to be interviewed about their claim for income support. £250m extra help announced for homeless people over two years.

December: New regulations come in excluding claims for unemployment benefit from people earning over lower earnings limit.

1990

January: Social Security Bill published giving pension proposals, and some disability benefit measures, including abolition of earnings-related invalidity benefit. Prime Minister launches drive to make fathers pay maintenance for their children. National insurance fund will be £1.7bn in deficit in 1990/91, due mainly to contribution refunds to people contracting out of state earnings-related pension scheme. Announcement of government proposals on disability benefits.

February: High Court judgment on social fund that guidance on local office budgets is defective. Report shows 40 per cent fall in prescriptions dispensed due to price rises. Fewer than 1 per cent of unemployed claimants interviewed under Restart are placed in jobs.

March: Budget: capital limits for poll tax rebates and housing benefit to be doubled; government forced to backdate for Scotland. Workplace nurseries no longer taxed as benefit in kind for employees. Social fund budget increased by £10m (from loan repayments). Government

announces extra £50m for poll tax transitional relief scheme. Independent Living Fund, set up to help disabled people, runs out of money (but is later saved). Government says average poll tax will be £363; about 10m people will get rebates. Measures announced to enforce maintenance payments.

April: Child benefit frozen for third year running. Prescription charges up to £3.05. Poll tax comes in in England and Wales. Capital limits for means-tested benefits raised. Independent taxation implemented. Rules tightened for unemployed people on benefit. Major mistakes revealed in government poverty figures: poorest 10 per cent of population had only half average income growth in 1982-85 (*see* May 1988). Virtual freeze in social fund budget.

May: Social Services Committee says government statistics on low incomes are unsatisfactory and misleading; its report shows 12.2m people on or below income support levels in 1987.

June: Government announces plans to deduct maintenance direct from wages before liable parents default.

July: Government *Households below Average Income 1981-1987* statistics show incomes after housing costs of poorest 10 per cent went up only 0.1 per cent between 1979 and 1987 in comparison with 23 per cent for average. Social Security Bill denies housing benefit to students.

August: Record levels of mortgage arrears and repossessions of homes reported. British Medical Journal shows health gap between rich and poor widened in last ten years. National Audit Office report shows doubling in numbers of homeless people since 1987.

September: Government issues new directions and guidance for social fund to reassert control of local office budgets.

October: £10 premium for carers on income support. Disregard for lone parents on housing benefit increased. White Paper on maintenance published (*see* July 1991).

November: Criminal Justice Bill published, containing plans to deduct fines direct from benefit. John Major is new Prime Minister, promoting vision of classless society. Disability Benefits Bill published, proposing new disability living allowance and disability working allowance.

December: Severe disablement allowance age-related additions introduced. Restart courses compulsory for some long-term unemployed (40 per cent cut in benefit for refusal). Government promises 1,000 beds in London for homeless people.

1991

January: New Commons Select Committee on Social Security established.

February: Job-start programme (top-up of low wages for long-term unemployed taking jobs) to be scrapped. Cold weather payments increased from £5 to £6 per week and rule on seven consecutive days' freeze temporarily waived. National Audit Office report on social fund criticises inconsistency in decisions and multiple indebtedness for claimants. Court of Appeal rules Secretary of State within his rights in depriving around 400,000 people of severe disability premium.

March: Budget: £140 deduction from poll tax bills to be financed by rise in VAT from 15 to 17.5 per cent; child benefit to be increased from October by another £1 for first/only child (to £9.25) and for others by 25p (to £7.50) and to be index-linked from April 1992; claimants on income support and family credit to get

identical increases; freeze on married couple's allowance, one parent benefit and lone parents' additional tax allowance. Extra £55m announced by government to help unemployed. Chief Adjudication Officer's report published, with criticism of quality of DSS decision-making.

April: Uprating week: most non-means-tested benefits go up by 10.9 per cent and means-tested benefits by 8.1 per cent. Child benefit £1 per week higher for first or eldest child, but frozen at £7.25 for others. One parent benefit frozen. Major reforms of NHS introduced: self-governing trusts, purchaser/provider split, internal markets. New Benefits Agency and Contributions Agency launched. Income support and housing benefit for people in residential care and nursing homes paid under similar rules to those for people in own homes. Prescription charges up to £3.40. *Breadline Britain* survey shows more than 11 million living in poverty, defined as lacking three or more necessities. Council tax plans announced, with 100 per cent rebates to be reintroduced: likely implementation date 1993/94.

May: Minister for Disabled People announces DSS will create successor body to Independent Living Fund in 1993. Social Security Committee report shows 2 per cent rise in incomes of poorest tenth between 1979 and 1988, compared to 33.5 per cent rise for average; between 1979 and 1988 numbers below half average income grew to 11.8 million – from 9.4 per cent of population to 21.6 per cent; proportion of children in households below half average income doubled to one in four. White Paper on education proposes training credits for all 16-17-year-olds leaving full-time education.

June: Consultation paper on legal aid published. Cold weather payments to be changed: can be paid on forecast of freeze for 7 days; and to be automatic, without application. Benefits Enquiry Line launched for people with disabilities. Government to consult on how to achieve equal treatment between men and women in state pension scheme. Disability Living Allowance and Disability Working Allowance Act receives Royal Assent; new benefits to be introduced in April 1992

(*see* November 1990).

July: Citizen's Charter launched, promising better standards in public services and rights to redress. Child Support Act receives Royal Assent, setting stage for new system of child maintenance and establishment of Child Support Agency (*see* October 1990).

Entries from June 1979 – April 1987 are slightly edited versions of those included in 'Mrs Thatcher's Diary' by Ann Stanyer in *Thatcherism and the Poor* (edited by David Bull and Paul Wilding, CPAG, 1983) and by Huw Edwards in *The Growing Divide* (edited by Alan Walker and Carol Walker, CPAG Ltd, 1987).

CONSUMING CREDIT

CHILD POVERTY ACTION GROUP

Debt and poverty in the UK

Janet Ford

Consuming Credit examines the links between increased poverty, the growth of the credit industry and the problems of debt.

Issues examined include:
- the exclusion of the poor from some forms of credit, and how they are channelled into higher cost repayment schemes
- the concentration of debt amongst the poor
- the social and personal consequences of debt
- the burden that falls on women
- protection for credit users
- remedies

'The strength of Janet Ford's study is her success in documenting a wide variety of material on credit and debt and combining this with an analysis of how poverty causes debt, rather than vice versa ... the study brings together divergent sources in an accessible format.' – *Roof*

'It should be compulsory reading for Government.' – *Frontline:* Social Welfare Law Quarterly, NI

| 128 pages | 1991 | 0 946744 32 7 | £5.95 |

Please send me _____ copy/ies of *Consuming Credit* @ £5.95 each (incl p&p) £_____

I enclose a donation of £_____ towards CPAG's work

I enclose a cheque/PO for £_____, payable to CPAG Ltd

Name _____

Address _____

_____

_____ Postcode _____

Return payment with order to CPAG Ltd, 1-5 Bath Street, London EC1V 9PY

POVERTY: THE FACTS

Carey Oppenheim

CHILD POVERTY ACTION GROUP

Poverty: the facts presents the latest statistics on the nature and extent of poverty in the UK. This new and fully updated edition has been much expanded to include fuller coverage of such topics as: debates on the definition of poverty; government and other statistics; causes and consequences of poverty; poverty in relation to race and gender; deprivation in Scotland, Wales, Northern Ireland and in the English regions; international comparisons.

Fully illustrated with graphs, tables, maps and photographs, *Poverty: the facts* is the most comprehensive, authoritative and accessible assessment of poverty in contemporary Britain.

160 pages   1990   0 946744 28 9   £5.95

- -

Please send me _____ copy/ies of *Poverty: the facts* @ £5.95 each (incl p&p) £_____

I enclose a donation of £_____ towards CPAG's work

I enclose a cheque/PO for £_____, payable to CPAG Ltd

Name_____

Address_____

_____

_____

_____ Postcode_____

Please send cash with order to CPAG Ltd, 1-5 Bath Street, London EC1V 9PY

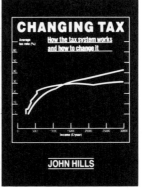

Now's the time to join CPAG!

CHILD POVERTY ACTION GROUP

We can help you ... with the facts on poverty.

You can help us ... in the fight against poverty.

CPAG membership gives you access to all the latest – on welfare rights, income inequalities, perspectives on policy, and lots more!

And CPAG members give us the support we need to ensure that poverty is at the heart of the agenda, whatever political party is in power.

Send off the form and join CPAG now.

Please complete and send to:
CPAG, 4th Floor, 1-5 Bath Street, London EC1V 9PY

❏ I would like to join CPAG as a comprehensive member £40
(Comprehensive members receive CPAG's regular journal, *Poverty,* plus welfare rights and social policy publications)
or

❏ I would like information about other membership options

❏ I enclose a donation to CPAG of £_____

❏ I enclose a cheque/PO (made out to CPAG) for £_____

Name_____

Organisation (if applicable) _____

Address_____

_____

_____ Postcode_____